BLOOD
from a
STONE

BLOOD
from a
STONE

THE QUEST FOR
THE LIFE DIAMONDS

Yaron Svoray
and
Richard Hammer

A Tom Doherty Associates Book
New York

BLOOD FROM A STONE: THE QUEST FOR THE LIFE DIAMONDS

This book is printed on acid-free paper.

Edited by Patrick LoBrutto

Book design by Michael Collica

A Forge Book
Published by Tom Doherty Associates, LLC
175 Fifth Avenue
New York, NY 10010

www.tor.com

Forge® is a registered trademark of Tom Doherty Associates, LLC.

Library of Congress Cataloging-in-Publication Data

Svoray, Yaron.
Blood from a stone: the quest for the life diamonds /
Yaron Svoray and Richard Hammer.
p. cm.
ISBN 0-765-30795-2
1. Holocaust, Jewish (1939–1945)—Economic aspects—Germany. 2. World War, 1939–1945—Economic aspects—Germany. 3. World War, 1939–1945—Confiscations and contributions—Germany. 4. Diamonds—Germany—History—20th century. 5. Jewish property—Germany. I. Hammer, Richard, 1928– II. Title.

D804.7.E26S85 2003
940.53'1813—dc21
2002045456

First Edition: May 2003

Printed in the United States of America

0 9 8 7 6 5 4 3 2 1

For the Children

Contents

CONTENTS

Acknowledgments

This book could not have been written without the assistance of a great many people with expertise in certain areas, and many in the United States, France, Germany, the Netherlands, Israel, and elsewhere who opened their memories, some, especially survivors of the Holocaust, with considerable reluctance and only on the promise of anonymity. Some, with their permission, are mentioned in the body of this work and so will not be cited again here. The names of others have been changed at their request.

In the discussion of diamonds, the authors are grateful for the help provided by Dr. George E. Harlow, curator of minerals and gems at the American Museum of Natural History and one of the world's foremost experts on diamonds, and the volume he edited, *The Nature of Diamonds*. In addition, we relied heavily on Eric Bruton's classic study, *Diamonds*, Jacques Legrand's *Diamonds: Myth, Magic and Reality*, and Stefan Kanfer's *The Last Empire: De Beers, Diamonds and the World*.

On the plight of the Jews in the Middle Ages, among the sources were Barbara W. Tuchman's *A Distant Mirror*, Johan Huizinga's *The Waning of the Middle Ages*, David Herlihy's *Medieval Culture and Society*, J. B. Ross and M. M. McLaughlin's *The Portable Medieval Reader*, and Israel Abraham's *Jewish Life in the Middle Ages*.

The major sources on the Holocaust in addition to the personal recollections of survivors included the Yad Vashem Holocaust Museum and Memorial in Jerusalem, the Simon Wiesenthal Center in Los Angeles, the Holocaust Museum in Washington, the Museum of Tolerance Multimedia Learning Center, the Jewish Student Online Research Center, Lucy Dawidowicz's *The War Against the Jews, 1933–1945*, Martin Gilbert's *The Holocaust: A History of the Jews of Europe During the Second World War*, I. J. Blanken's *The History of Philips Electronics NV: Under German Rule*, Yehuda Svoray's *The Shipwrecked Camel*, and many others too numerous to mention. In the sections on the concentration camps at Majdanek and Auschwitz II–Birkenau, we used the personal recollections of two survivors of each camp, not because they were unique but as representatives of the thousands of children and teenagers forced to labor for the Nazis.

For details on the movement of the U.S. Seventh Army after its landing in the summer of 1944 on the Mediterranean coast of France, we relied on official U.S. Army records and summations as well as a variety of studies of the war, including information contained in the Web sites of various units of the Seventh Army.

Finally, we must note the continuing and enthusiastic support of and belief in this work by Mel Berger, our agent at the William Morris Agency, who played a role in the journey's culmination; Alan Kannof, head of the New York office of the William Morris Agency, who was instrumental in bringing the authors together and who believed in this story so strongly that he helped finance the "End of the Journey"; and Donna Bagdasarian of William Morris who provided comfort, understanding, and help without complaint. And, without the total support of our wives, Mikhal Svoray and Arlene Hammer, who read this book in manuscript and offered invaluable criticism and suggestions, and our families, we could never have completed this work.

To all, we offer our appreciation.

Prologue

Life Diamonds they were called. Large, uncut stones—rough diamonds of the best quality. Bought by wealthy Jews in Eastern Europe during the first decades of the twentieth century, they were supposed to serve as protection, a passport to safety and a new life when peril descended.

Death Diamonds they became after 1939, when the Third Reich conquered Poland, and, especially after the middle of 1941, when the Nazi blitzkrieg raced through the Balkans and invaded the Soviet Union, and the Third Reich established a network of extermination camps in the conquered territories of Eastern Europe.

This is the story of the journey of forty of those Life Diamonds across oceans and continents, from the mines of South Africa to the diamond centers in Amsterdam and Antwerp, to the cities and ghettos and shtetls of Eastern Europe, to the death camps in the East, then back to the Netherlands, on to Strasbourg and adjacent communities, and finally to a small pit in the side of one foxhole in a forest on a hill in Alsace on the border between France and Germany. It is the story of those who possessed them, those who wanted them, those forced to relinquish them, those compelled to search for them, those who appraised them, those who transported them, those who died for them, and of two American soldiers who liberated them from Nazi SS officers and then buried them in that foxhole. It is the story of how and why diamonds became the most treasured, and in some ways the most feared, of man's possessions. It is, too, the story of one man, Yaron Svoray, who spent more than a decade in search of that foxhole, in search of those Life Diamonds, whose own life was unalterably changed by that search, far beyond his own imagining. And it is the story of the curse that some said lay over them, bringing death and disaster to all who imagined they owned them.

What began in 1988 as a treasure hunt by an Israeli, Yaron Svoray, simply to enrich himself, led after nearly a dozen years to something far greater, far more momentous and life-altering. It led back more than half a century, to the Holocaust and the plunder ripped from Jewish victims.

It led, too, into the memories of an aging World War II veteran who had buried the forty diamonds and had not forgotten the smallest detail about where they were. But following the clues he offered led only to a series of hills, to a thousand square miles of forest with an untold number of foxholes in Alsace on the border between France and Germany. And the trail seemed never to lead to the right foxhole, to the place where those forty Life Diamonds had rested all through the years. It would take more than clues and more than dedication, more than obsession, to find the answer.

This, then, is the story of the journey in search of the answers that would unlock the puzzle.

That search came to a conclusion over a weekend in July 1999. After scores of trips to the Alsatian hills and forests through the years, after hundreds of hours of digging into foxholes dating back to World War I and finding nothing but rusted and deteriorated relics of the world wars, Svoray had come to a fateful decision. He would make one last attempt to unearth the diamonds. If he failed this time, as he had always failed in the past, he would abandon his quest, would leave the diamonds to rest in peace where they had been interred for more than half a century, and would try to pick up the threads of his life.

And so on that overcast, chill July weekend, Svoray and seven friends slogged up a steep hill named Kopfberg, along muddy lanes, and entered the forest for a final time.

PART I

The Journey of the Diamonds

1

First Words

"I want to tell you a story," the old man said.

Yaron Svoray sighed. The year was 1988 and Svoray, a former detective for Yamar, the Israeli equivalent of the FBI, was then studying for a master's degree in film studies and communications at Queens College in New York. A burly, bullet-headed man who, he often said, looked like a Turkish wrestler, he was supplementing his meager income by writing articles for an Israeli newspaper and by traveling around the United States lecturing on Middle Eastern politics and terrorism. After every lecture someone invariably approached him and wanted to tell him a story. This particular night he was in Bangor, Maine, when the old man cornered him. Svoray looked for an escape, but there didn't seem to be one.

"Listen," the old man, whose name, Svoray learned, was Sam Nyer, persisted. "I want to tell you about two kids, one a tall, skinny, eighteen-year-old Jew from Brooklyn by way of Boston, and the other a little seventeen-year-old runt of an Indian from New Mexico or some other godforsaken place somewhere out in the West, and how they found a satchel full of treasure worth fifty, maybe a hundred million dollars." The old man looked at Svoray, grinned, and nodded knowingly. "So, now you're interested." It was a statement, not a question.

"I'll listen," Svoray said without committing himself further.

The old man dug his fingers into Svoray's arm. "It's a long story," he said. "I hope you have time."

At the center of his story was a purple leather pouch on which were embossed gold letters, a pouch that contained forty uncut, rough diamonds, and the curse that Sam Nyer said hovered over those stones.

It was a story that would send Svoray on an eleven-year mission in search not merely of those buried gems but, though it was years before he understood it, in search of himself.

2

Origins

Svoray was about to discover what Sam Nyer had already learned, to his sorrow, and what men from time immemorial had learned—that the quest for diamonds, and the riches they could bring, was arduous and fraught with peril, and possession of those gems brought not only wealth but the potential for disaster.

Diamonds are unique. Of all nature's treasures, man has attributed curses only to diamonds, not rubies nor emeralds nor sapphires nor gold. Of all nature's treasures, man has given proper identifying names only to diamonds, not rubies nor emeralds nor sapphires nor gold. The names borne by some of the largest diamonds are instantly recognizable, resound, call up images, echo with fabulous and fantastic stories, have traceable histories—the Hope, the Regent, the Koh-i-Nor, the Sancy, the Tiffany, the Orlov, the Great Mogul, the Cullinan, the Dresden Green, the Kasikie, the Centenary, the Shah Jahan, and dozens more. And some are said to carry a curse.

The fascination with diamonds, and the idea that some—particularly the biggest, the most beautiful, the most valuable—might be cursed, was probably born within moments of man's realization that those fiery, incredibly hard, incandescent stones found in streambeds and other out-of-the-way places, initially on the Indian subcontinent, were something extraordinary, like nothing else in nature. That moment, according to the best estimates, was sometime near the beginning to middle of the first millennium B.C.E., and the people who found the first diamonds must have marveled at their discovery and wondered whence those brilliant stones could have come. Those stones were, and are, the hardest natural substance known to man, can cut through any other substance with nearly the ease of a knife through soft butter, but can themselves be cut or even scratched only by another diamond. Those stones were, and remain, the most beautiful, the most valuable and valued, the most desired of all natural substances.

More than two thousand years later, in the age of scientific discovery, the answer emerged. Created from carbon under extreme pressure over millions of years in the earth's mantle, hundreds of miles beneath the surface, then propelled toward the earth's crust in widening, funnel-shaped pipes by volcanic eruptions, most are embedded in a dense, hard, blue layer called kimberlite, deep within the earth's crust. Others come to rest closer to the surface in a loose, yellowish soil, and a smaller number are washed away over centuries by torrential rains and end up in distant alluvial deposits, mixing with gravel and other minerals in gullies, ravines, and streambeds, waiting to be discovered.

Yet without the benefit of scientific knowledge, other explanations had to be found in those ancient times. In India, the myths of creation arose along with the belief that, unlike nearly all other natural substances, magical properties were inherent in these gems, magic for good and magic for evil, beneficence and curse. If they were, as people then believed, a great and wonderful gift from the gods, then it followed that they could not be an unalloyed gift, that some must also contain evil.

Myth, legend, history, and literature are filled with stories of cursed diamonds, dating back to the earliest recorded times.

In Sanskrit they were called *vajra*, "thunderbolt," and *indra-yudha*, "Indira's weapon," and the first written mention of diamonds appears in a Sanskrit text from about 300 B.C.E., hundreds of years after the initial discovery. The best diamonds, the text says, were "hexagonal, square or round, of flashing color, having a suitable form, clear, smooth, lustrous, with lustre inside and imparting lustre."

And a myth surrounds their creation. There was a great but evil king named Bala, so powerful that even the gods could not defeat him in battle. So the gods devised a scheme to destroy him. They proposed that as a favor to the highest powers, in order to gain a measure of redemption, he offer himself as a ritual sacrifice. He agreed, and he was tied to a stake by thirteen strings and then consumed by fire. His ashes turned into diamonds; some the gods carried away while others fell to earth in seven places—the Gulf of Cambay in northwest India, the Kalinga coast on the Bay of Bengal, the Veinganga River in the Chandra district, Behar, Ayodhya, the Ganges plain, and Golconda—though a legend arose of an eighth location, the mythical Valley of Diamonds somewhere in the Himalayas. For the next two thousand years, these were only known sources of diamonds.

Still, if diamonds were a gift from the gods, they were not a gift for everyone. They were a gift reserved for the royal, the rich, and the powerful. And even for them, there were gradations. Most diamonds are brilliant and colorless. Colored diamonds are rare, remarkable, only one in ten thousand, so they are the most prized and the most expensive. Thus, in India, and later as diamonds were discovered in other places, only a king could possess a red or a yellow diamond. Gems of other colors, down to the colorless, were reserved for descending orders of the powerful, while the lower castes could own only flawed stones that were used for drilling, cutting, polishing, and other industrial purposes.

Like all gifts from the gods, though, diamonds came with a catch. Some were filled with good attributes, which were taken on by those who came to possess or own them. Good diamonds, it was believed, could destroy evil spirits, neutralize poison, slay serpents, cure sickness, banish sins of all kinds. But they had to be found in the right places at the right time, under the right sign. If not, then they were cursed, became evil, were filled with fatal influences and stripped of all beneficial qualities. And there were those who were also convinced that since diamonds were the ashes of the evil king Bala, an evil curse was somehow attached to all diamonds, no matter where or when they were found, no matter how perfect.

For those who prized them, though, the notion that evil might pervade all of them, that they all might be cursed, was dismissed out of hand. The *Ratnapariska* (*Examination of Precious Stones*) of Buddha Bhatta, a manual written in the fifth century C.E., declares, "He who, having pure body, always carries a diamond with sharp points, without blemish, free from all faults; that one, as long as he lives, knows each day will bear some things: happiness, prosperity, children, riches, grain, cows, and meat. He who wears such a diamond will see danger recede from him whether he be threatened by serpents, fire, poison, sickness, thieves, flood, or evil spirits." The diamond with a blemish, even a small one, even though barely perceptible, "should not be carried by those who desire happiness in this world . . . a diamond having a portion with the color of blood or that is glittering with red spots will quickly bring death to the carrier, even to the Master of death."

That diamonds were cursed was a myth, then, that began

almost with their discovery and has persisted down through the ages. One reason the notion was concocted—but only one— was as a way to deter fortune hunters. The biggest, the best, the most beautiful diamonds carried a curse, and those who would steal them or try somehow to possess them had better beware. Stories of the cursed stones were passed from generation to generation and came to be accepted as gospel. Eventually, the lure of diamonds was seen to be fraught with peril.

That conviction, that some diamonds might be cursed, grew, spread, and flourished. Perhaps the first curse, and one of the most famous, was that of the Koh-i-Nor, the "Mountain of Light." It was, of course, only one among many. Curses hung over the Regent, the Orlov, the Great Mogul, the Hope, and dozens more, and ill fortune seemed to follow those who possessed them. (For the stories of the famous cursed diamonds, see Appendix A.)

3

Moving West

For two thousand years, India was alone in possession of diamonds. Laws were promulgated forbidding their export. But as word reached the outside world of these gems, there were those determined to profit by a valuable trade. Rules and laws could not prevent it, and soon new laws were laid down detailing pricing, though still banning the sale of the most precious stones. Trade developed between India and China and Persia, never on a large scale, since production of diamonds in India never exceeded 50,000 to 100,000 carats in any one year, and averaged about 10,000 carats a year, only a small percentage of gem quality. But the lure of diamonds as adornments of the powerful, and as symbolic decorations embedded in images of the gods, drew travelers from the outside world seeking whatever they could make away with, by purchase or theft.

Legend has it that the first European to come upon diamonds was Alexander the Great during his invasion of India across the Himalayas around 327 B.C.E. Rumors had already spread to the West about these fantastic stones, which the Greeks called *adamas*, meaning "extreme hardness" (which is probably the root of the old French *diamant* and the fifteenth-century English *dyamaund*). According to Aristotle, and later Pliny the Elder, Alexander discovered a deep valley, more like a chasm, that was so steep no one could descend it, at the bottom of which were diamonds guarded by serpents whose Medusa-like image brought death to anyone who looked at them. Alexander destroyed the serpents by forcing them to look at their reflections in iron mirrors; then, on the advice of wise men, threw pieces of flesh into the chasm. The diamonds became attached to the meat, birds swooped down and carried the diamond-encrusted flesh out of the valley, and Alexander gathered the vast treasure.

The myth of the Valley of Diamonds, echoed in the tales of the third voyage of Sinbad the Sailor and of the travels of Marco Polo, is undoubtedly no more than a myth dreamed up by Indian diamond merchants in Golconda. Their purpose in promulgating the myth was to send diamond hunters on a wild-goose chase away from the true sources of the gems in the riverbeds of the surrounding countryside, just as they invented other fabrications to discourage outsiders.

Diamonds were so hard, they declared, that they could not be damaged when struck by any implement. Pliny the Elder bought into this concept when he wrote, "The stones are tested upon an anvil, and will resist any blow to such an extent as to make the iron rebound and the very anvil split asunder."

The reality, which was not grasped for centuries, is that the very hardness of diamonds also makes them brittle, so they can be crushed, shattered into pieces, if hit with a hammer in the right way. Charles the Bold, Duke of Burgundy, lost a fortune after the battle of Morat in 1476 when Swiss mercenaries smashed a collection of diamonds with hatchets and hammers to see if they were real; and when the stones were turned to powder, they left the debris on the battlefield in disgust, to be gathered by those who realized what they were collecting, and who turned those collections into small fortunes.

Even as late as the nineteenth century, the belief in the invulnerability of diamonds persisted. Miners and other adventurers at the diamond finds in South Africa accepted this as fact, so ingenious diamond merchants would frequently shatter stones and persuade the miners that what they had found were not real diamonds; the miners would walk away disconsolate, and the merchants would walk away with the pieces of real diamonds.

It was centuries before diamonds began to flow in any number to the West, beyond Persia to Europe. In Europe, however, the rise of Christianity made diamonds anathema. The reason: Christianity's initial dedication to a simple life, to the purity of the spirit and the rejection of lavish adornments—anything that was linked to what was considered pagan culture and mysticism. It was not until the waning days of the Middle Ages, when Christianity was securely entrenched in European society and fears were fading that people would be burned at the stake for heresy at the slightest show of interest in the more exotic indulgences of the East, that diamonds became the desired objects of monarchs and nobles and the rich.

4

Diamonds and Jews

European society was changing. Disjointed, isolated, self-sufficient settlements and developing city-states began to spread out and make contact with their neighbors, near and far. They began to trade, dropped self-sufficiency, and became interdependent. In the process, a natural rivalry developed and grew, not merely between the new realms but between the secular rulers and the church in Rome. The new leaders desired earthly treasures and lavish ornaments to mark their power, wealth, and position, while the church continued to preach the doctrine of poverty—that it was easier for a camel to pass through the eye of a needle than for a rich man to enter the kingdom of heaven—of simplicity, of the spiritual life. Wealth, in the form of gems and other adornments, was seen as inexorably linked to the pagan East; even the church fathers themselves were not above gathering those possessions for themselves and for their church.

As this new order was being born, the old order was passing into history. No longer did every man have his unchanging and unchangeable place (the peasant remaining forever the peasant and the king and his progeny remaining the rulers, with those in between locked in their anointed stations). A certain mobility, the capacity to rise somewhere on a higher scale, was now the rule rather than the exception. In the towns and cities guilds arose, uniting the tradesmen with common interests, giving them a power they had never before attained. A youth could become an apprentice to the guild of silversmiths, leather workers, weavers, metalworkers, tailors, shoemakers, bakers, millers, carpenters, goldsmiths—any one of a dozen guilds controlling the trades—and rise to become a master.

But barred from the guilds, barred from any role in this emerging society, were the Jews, those stateless people wandering in the Diaspora, always at the mercy of whim and chance, the momentary or ongoing precepts of church and state. They were rarely safe, never permanent residents, never citizens, forever subject to sudden expulsion and the expropriation of everything they owned. They were anathema. They were blamed for every ill that befell society, from the plague to the contamination of wells and water supplies. They were the Christ killers. They were accused of ritual murder. They were forbidden to employ a Christian or to sue a Christian; to serve as doctors; to deliver or receive goods; to sell flour, bread, wine, oil, shoes, any article of clothing, or anything society considered essential; to hold land or claim it as payment for a debt. They were forced to wear a yellow circular badge to signify that they were Jews. In 1205, Pope Innocent III, with the backing of Thomas Aquinas, enunciated the doctrine that Jews were doomed to perpetual servitude because they had killed Christ, and, as Aquinas put it in *The Kingdom of God,* "since Jews are the slaves of the Church, She can dispense of their possessions."

How, then, could a Jew, essentially barred from every aspect of life, survive in this Christian society bent on his isolation and eventual destruction? Without realizing the implications, the church and the monarchs opened the door just a crack, and those Jews who sensed it and had the talent and foresight to seize the opportunity, stepped through. The church had condemned moneylending, the use of money to make money. For a Christian to lend money at interest was a mortal sin. Therefore, a societal order came into being where the Jews would lend money at interest, as much as 20 percent or more, to the Christians desperate for it. Hence Antonio, Shakespeare's merchant of Venice, his money tied up in his ships at sea, is forced to go to the only available source for needed funds to help his friend, Bassanio. That source was the moneylender Shylock. What Shakespeare skimmed over, though, and what the common man was not aware of, was that the royal treasury raked in most of the interest in the form of taxation, and that wealthy Christians, forbidden to lend at interest, financed the Jewish bankers in their lending operations and then took in most of the profits. And, all too often, that was not enough. When the crown required ever more money to finance burgeoning activities, it simply ordered the expulsion of the Jews and seized their money and property.

But this was the wedge that eventually led to the rise of the court Jews, the Rothschilds and other financiers who guided the monarchs of Europe to wealth and power, and, in the process, gained a measure of power for themselves.

And then there were diamonds—those gems whose source was in polytheistic, idol-worshipping India and whose possession, thus, was considered a sin, though a sin that came increasingly to be ignored. As glittering, costly possessions became ever more desired and sought by the princes and the rich, the demand grew, and since the supply was limited, the value increased. But initially there was no diamond guild, so dealing in diamonds was an activity not barred to Jews, who quickly moved into dominant positions.

Until the fourteenth century, almost all diamonds were rough, uncut stones. Cutting and polishing were relatively unknown, though there had been some attempts in India to polish diamonds using the powder resulting from the crushing of other diamonds. But the Indian dealers warned that once a diamond was polished, it lost all its magical powers.

In Europe, though, the beauty that resulted from polishing made diamonds even more desirable, and the idea of lost magic was dismissed as pagan hokum. Initially, Venice was the diamond center of Europe, the stones traveling overland from the Indian mines. There, shortly after 1330, the art of polishing came into wide use and spread across Europe over the next century. It took root in Antwerp, which grew rapidly as the city became the continent's diamond center when the Portuguese discovered a direct sea route to India. In Antwerp, the art of grading diamonds, from gem quality down to bort industrial stones, was refined, and diamond cutting—using a whole piece of a diamond, rather than just the diamond dust, to shape, facet, and polish another diamond—emerged around 1550.

When the Spanish attacked Antwerp in 1585, the diamond trade fled, establishing a new center in Amsterdam to the north. Into this new diamond capital came the Jews—with a talent for appraising and cutting—who had been expelled from Spain by the Inquisition. They settled in the Netherlands where there were few barriers to their practicing this new craft.

Diamonds had a particular attraction for the Jews, and not merely because so few walls had been erected to prevent them from dealing in every aspect of the precious gems. They were valuable, their value growing with the limited supply. They were in demand, the demand increasing. And they were small, which meant that, unlike gold or other valuable items, they could be easily hidden and easily transported and easily turned into money. Diamonds were emerging as a new international currency, valued everywhere. They were becoming a form of protection, a hedge against the rise and fall in the value of local currencies. They transcended national boundaries. And they were not forbidden to the Jews. For a people who lived wherever they settled only on the sufferance of the princes, who could be thrown out at a moment's notice, the portability, the international value, the ease of convertibility were of prime importance. This view of diamonds as a hedge against fate would last to the present.

5

A New Discovery

Until early in the eighteenth century, the flow of rough diamonds continued at a steady pace to the dealers, appraisers, and cutters in Antwerp and Amsterdam from the mines of India. Then, almost without warning, the supply dipped sharply. Diamonds from the Indian mines became scarcer and scarcer, only an average of 2,000 to 5,000 carats arriving in Europe annually. The mines were nearing exhaustion; the same ground had been sifted again and again in the vain hope of new discoveries. Prices rose sharply as merchants suspected that the diamonds on hand would be all there ever were. For the appraisers and the cutters, it was a bleak moment. If there were to be no more diamonds, then there would be dwindling work for them.

In 1725, all that changed. According to legend, Sebastino Leme do Prado, a Portuguese official, came upon a group of gold prospectors playing cards and using bright crystalline stones as chips near the Rio dos Marinhos in the present-day province of Minas Gerais in Brazil. Leme do Prado, who had lived in India before arriving in Brazil, was convinced the stones were diamonds, and he was told that there were hundreds, perhaps thousands of similar stones in the area's riverbeds. The stones were gathered and by 1727 enough had been accumulated to send them to Lisbon and then on to Amsterdam to be appraised. They were, indeed, diamonds.

More diamonds were discovered in alluvial gold deposits near the town of Tejuca, soon renamed Diamantina, and then additional finds were made in a number of other locations in Brazil. Diamond prospectors poured into Brazil, sifted through the surface soil, dug deeper; and more than a few walked out rich men.

In the diamond centers of Europe, the Brazilian finds were good news, and bad. The good news was, of course, that the feared end of the diamond trade was not imminent. The bad news for the diamond dealers was that the influx of diamonds from Brazil, reaching 50,000 to 100,000 carats a year, coupled with a conviction that the supply in Brazil was practically end-less and could be exploited with little effort, resulted in a glut and the collapse of diamond prices. By 1735, the price had declined to just 25 percent of what it had been only a decade earlier. The Portuguese government stepped into the chaotic market situation and, in an effort to stabilize prices, sharply restricted production and then declared mining a royal monop-oly.

But so extensively were the Brazilian deposits worked over that, in about a century and a quarter, by the 1860s, they were in danger of being depleted, as the Indian deposits before them. Once more, there was a serious diamond shortage in the cutting centers and a growing fear that the diamond trade was coming to an end.

6

The Greatest Discovery

In February 1867, Erasmus Jacobs, a fifteen-year-old Boer, picked up a glittering pebble on a gravel bank on the De Kalk farm on the southern bank of the Orange River in South Africa's Cape Province. That pebble turned out to be a 10.73-carat diamond, and it led to the greatest diamond rush and the greatest and richest diamond finds in history, and changed South Africa from a backward society and a costly drain on the British Empire's treasury into the most prized jewel in Queen Victoria's crown. It had taken India two thousand years to produce 21 million carats of diamonds, and Brazil two hundred years to produce that number of carats; in a mere fifteen years, from Erasmus Jacobs's find to 1882, South Africa had surpassed both.

The discovery also brought to the surface a virulent anti-Semitism. Until the Cape Province diamond finds, South Africa had been a relatively safe haven for Jews fleeing the prejudices, the pogroms, the anti-Semitism of Europe. If anti-Jewish sentiments were there, they tended to lurk beneath the surface, waiting to rise. But the settlers in this raw land, the Boers of Dutch descent and the English, were too busy trying to scratch out a meager existence from the barren, arid earth to devote much time and energy to anything else. Diamonds changed all that.

South Africans and Europeans were drawn by the prospects

of the untold riches lying on the surface and just beneath it. Raw towns began to spring up around the Orange, Riet, and Vaal Rivers—Kimberly, Bultfonten, De Beers, Dutoitspan, Wesselton, Patel, Jagersfontein, Hopetown, and the rest. Like others seeking the riches that seemed there for the taking, Jews headed for the diamond fields from their homes in Cape Town and from all over Europe. Most were just miners, content to sift the ground for gems and live and practice their religion unobtrusively, traveling on the High Holy Days to the nearest rabbis in synagogues hundreds of miles distant or in Cape Town.

But there were the flamboyant Jews who arrived to wheel and deal, buy diamonds at the lowest possible price, strike hard bargains, then sell at inflated prices and reap fortunes. "The Jews have got ahead of us again," complained some miners. A letter from one disappointed miner to a Cape Town newspaper declared, "Diamonds are cropping up fast and trade in these gems is now a firm fact; but the Jews up here are making efforts to keep the trade in their hands."

The bitterness grew with the arrival of a one-time Jewish vaudevillian named Barney Barnato in 1873. He had a keen eye for appraising rough, uncut diamonds and a talent for persuading the miners who found them to sell for what he offered. He branched out and started buying up claims. More often than not, the ones he bought turned out to be among the best and the richest, and within a few years he was one of the most important diamond moguls in South Africa, controlling the Kimberly Central Mining Company, the largest diamond producer at the time.

Barnato's ambition to seize control of the diamond fields and the diamond markets was matched by and brought him into intense conflict with another recent arrival, the equally ambitious and even more ruthless Cecil Rhodes. For years, they waged fierce battles for control of the diamond business, in the mine fields, in and out of the courts of South Africa, and in the boardrooms of major European banking houses. Rhodes eventually emerged victorious, and his De Beers Mining Company became the dominant player in the South African diamond industry; indeed, in the whole international diamond trade. (For the story of the bitter war for control of the diamond trade between Rhodes and Barnato, see Appendix B.)

The beginnings of the De Beers diamond monopoly, set in motion by Rhodes, were brought to fruition by Ernest Oppenheimer, a German Jew who had settled in London at the age of sixteen and gone to work for a diamond firm there, which dispatched him to South Africa as its representative. He rose rapidly, entrenched himself, and eventually became the industry's supreme ruler, controlling not merely De Beers but a parent company he founded, Anglo-American Corporation of South Africa, into which he folded De Beers as well as South Africa's gold mines and more.

One of his greatest coups was acquiring the controlling interest in 1917 in the Premier Mine, the most important rival to De Beers. Fifteen years earlier, he had gained a foothold in the Premier when Thomas Cullinan, a one-time Johannesburg brickworks proprietor, was trying to raise the money to purchase the Prinsloo farm, three hundred miles northeast of Kimberly and eighteen miles east of Pretoria, on which he had accidentally stumbled upon a glittering stone. The price of the farm was £52,000 and Cullinan did not have the cash. So he formed a company he called the Premier Transvaal Diamond Company and offered to sell shares in it. Most potential investors thought it was a scam and backed away. Not Ernest Oppenheimer. He persuaded his employer, over loud objections, to buy a small stake in Cullinan's venture.

That stake paid off a thousandfold and more, for the Premier turned out to be the largest diamond pipe ever discovered up to that time. In its first year of operations it produced 750,000 carats and it averaged about 2 million carats a year thereafter, with more than three hundred stones exceeding 100 carats. It was at the Premier on January 26, 1905, that the largest diamond ever unearthed was found, about thirty feet beneath the surface. It was a stone that became known as the Cullinan Diamond. It was a colorless, 3,106-carat diamond, as large as a fist; it was so large its weight could be measured not merely in carats but in pounds: It tipped the scales at 1.37 pounds, an unbelievable weight for a diamond. Cullinan, after displaying it both in Johannesburg and London, offered it for sale at £500,000. There were no takers. Finally General Louis Botha suggested that the Transvaal government buy it and present it to King Edward VII. Transvaal officials haggled, finally came up with a price of £150,000, and then took 60 percent of that back as taxes. The Cullinan was so large that it could not be cut and faceted like an ordinary diamond and it contained flaws that had to be removed. The only way to deal with it was the potentially risky cleaving technique, striking the diamond along the weakest points. If done right, the stone will split neatly into desirable parts that can then be cut, shaped, and polished. If done wrong, the gem will be destroyed. The task was handed to the I.J. Ascher firm in Amsterdam in 1908, and Joseph Ascher was given the job of cleaving the stone. Nine fragments resulted, ranging from the 550.2-carat, pear-shaped Cullinan I, named the Great Star of Africa, the largest-known colorless diamond, mounted into the redesigned British royal scepter, to the 317.4-carat, cushion-cut Cullinan II, called the Lesser Star of Africa, mounted in the British imperial state crown, all the way down to a 4.80-carat, pear-shaped gem. Aside from the two Stars of Africa, the other cut stones were given to the Ascher firm as payment for its brilliant work. The company then sold some back to King Edward, who gave them as gifts to Queen Alexandra, and others to the Transvaal government, which presented them to the British royal family.

By 1917, Thomas Cullinan had gone on to other things, selling his interests in the Premier, but the mine continued to turn out vast numbers of gems and so ranked as a major threat to De Beers' monopolistic dreams. Oppenheimer dealt with that threat by simply buying enough stock in the Premier to lard it into De Beers. Gaining control of the Premier, then, was indeed a masterstroke by Ernest Oppenheimer. He was the richest man and the most important financial figure in South Africa. He was also ruthless, if not as ruthless as Rhodes, letting nothing stand in the way of attaining his goals. At the same time, he was one of the most charitable men of the early twentieth century. He funded schools, colleges, hospitals, and more, for both white and black Africans. But all his good works did little to combat the troubles and the prejudices he faced.

Though he later converted to Christianity, all his life he was the target of anti-Semitism. He was "Hoggenheimer," caricatured in newspapers and on the vaudeville stage as a Johannesburg Fagin, ruining everything he touched, stealing everything that was not nailed down, a predator who, when he was knighted, was accused of having bought his title.

Oppenheimer's business goal had been the creation of an orderly diamond market, controlled by De Beers, and he achieved it. A central buying office was established in London to which all South African diamonds were sent. The diamond merchants from the centers in Antwerp, Amsterdam, and elsewhere were invited to attend the showings of the new gems, examine them, and then buy what was offered at the price Oppenheimer, and his successors, dictated. If the buyers objected, they were not invited again until they made amends. And through De Beers' advertising and promotion efforts, the idea took root that diamonds—abundant because of the steady, controlled flow and seemingly endless supply in South Africa—were for everybody, even those of modest means. Ad campaigns trumpeted the notion that diamonds were an investment in the future that would never lose its value, a dictum that came to embraced throughout the world. "A diamond is forever," proclaimed De Beers, and the public believed it. Demand continued to rise and rise, and those who bought were happy, and those who dealt in diamonds—the merchants, appraisers, cutters—were delirious. Never had business been so good, and there was every sign that it would continue to be good, and get even better.

7

The Camps

For the European Jews at the end of the nineteenth century and on into the twentieth, the availability of diamonds was the best possible news. Now it was not only the very rich who could buy these passports to safety and freedom. Anyone with money, and not all that much, could now afford to purchase a diamond and store it in safety somewhere so that in times of desperation, it would provide the means of escape. And in the diamond centers of Antwerp and Amsterdam, the major diamond merchants were Jews, so a Jew in the market for a gem was certain his coreligionists would not cheat him, would sell him the best diamond at the best possible price.

There were perils, of course. In Eastern Europe, where the danger of pogroms was ever present, the arrival of marauding Cossacks meant not merely the possibility, but the probability of death or, at the very least, expulsion and the loss of everything. One might hide diamonds in the hems of garments, in other secret places, but the pillaging Cossacks soon learned that valuables were being hidden and even where, and searched for them, seized them, and left the now destitute with no way out.

There had to be a better way. For the very rich, there was: rough, uncut diamonds. If you had one, there was no need to hide it; unless the invaders knew what they were looking for, the rough diamond might be indistinguishable from a lump of sugar or a piece in a child's collection of stones and pebbles. It would be overlooked. But rough, uncut diamonds were large, upwards of a couple of inches in diameter, and those of the best quality were expensive. You had to have sufficient funds to buy even one.

As the waves of anti-Semitism raced across Europe after the First World War, and the future looked increasingly bleak for the European Jews, the wealthy in Poland, the Soviet Union, the Balkans, and the Baltic republics began to send their agents to the diamond centers to bargain for an uncut diamond. After a purchase was made, the diamond was carried back and then hidden in plain sight. This was now the secure exit visa. There are even tales of shtetls and ghettos pooling their resources, hiring an agent, and sending him to Amsterdam to buy an uncut stone; and when he returned, entrusting that stone to the safekeeping of the rabbi. These rough stones were given a name. They were called Life Diamonds, for those who owned them believed that they would buy escape, they would buy freedom in a new world, and they would be the means to settle into a new life with the wherewithal to enjoy it.

Then the Nazis arrived. And the gates of hell swung open and the Jews of Europe were marched through them into Auschwitz, Treblinka, Sobibor, Belzec, Majdanek, and all the other killing centers. These were the Jews without diamonds and the Jews with their cut diamonds and the Jews with their Life Diamonds. There was no protection.

8

KZ Majdanek

On what was ironically called Chopin Street in the heart of *Konzentrationslager* (concentration camp) Majdanek, a mile and a quarter from the outskirts of Lublin in eastern Poland, stood a vast warehouse. It had been built in 1939 as a hangar for the Polish Air Force, an antiquated assemblage of aircraft ill-equipped and manned by pilots inadequately trained in modern warfare. That air force was destroyed on the ground by the Luftwaffe in the first hours after the German invasion on September 1, 1939, and the hangar remained empty, deteriorating in the midst of a weed-choked, never-finished airstrip for the next two years. Then, after the Nazi invasion of the Soviet Union in June 1941, the former airfield, and the 667 surrounding acres, were ringed with double-electrified barbed-wire fence on the direct orders of SS Reichsführer Heinrich Himmler and put to another use. Inside that fence, 22 flimsy barracks in 5 separate sections—one for women, one for men, one for Russian prisoners, one for hostages, one for children—7 gas chambers, a crematorium with 5 furnaces, 2 wooden gallows, and more than 150 other structures turned Majdanek into a city of death.

This was a phase in *Akton Reinhard*, the brainchild of Himmler's chief deputy, SS General Reinhard Heydrich, for whom it was named. Heydrich was assassinated in Prague, Czechoslovakia, in the spring of 1942 and, in reprisal, the town of Lidice was burned to the ground, its 199 boys and men slaughtered. But destruction of Lidice was not Heydrich's only legacy. There was Majdanek, the easternmost of the camps, and there were those other cities of death, some larger but all based on a similar model, throughout occupied Poland—Auschwitz II– Birkenau, Sobibor, Belzec, Treblinka, and more. Those camps, whose function had been formalized at the Wannsee Conference over which Heydrich had presided four months before his death, had only two purposes—(1) to provide slave labor for the German war machine and plunder for the Nazi hierarchy, and (2) to consummate the "Final Solution" to the Jewish problem and the problem of other designated sub-species. To make sure that those purposes were fulfilled to the limit, Majdanek was placed under the command of men experienced in carrying out those tasks. Otto Koch, the first commandant, had run Buchenwald; his successor, Max Koegel, had run Ravensbrück; he was followed by Hermann Florstedt, sent to Majdanek from command of the prisoners' department at Buchenwald; Dachau's commandant, Martin Weiss, was next; and his successor was Arthur Liebehenschel, who had learned his craft at Auschwitz. Before Majdanek was liberated by the advancing Soviet Army, 235,000 of the 300,000 prisoners sent to the death camp had perished.

At KZ Majdanek, close to that never-used airplane hangar, now a warehouse, were the barracks for the children. Every morning at dawn, a squad of those children was herded into the warehouse to begin a day of labor that would last until dark. Waiting for them were mountains of clothes, suitcases, packing crates, and the other belongings stripped from the newly arrived who had been torn from their homes all over Europe and transported to this final destination on the road to extermination. Waiting, too, were the piles of hair, and gold and silver teeth, ripped from the dead.

On the orders of SS Lieutenant General August Frank, the commandants of all the extermination camps were told precisely what to do with the "property of the evacuated Jews." Foreign currency; jewelry; diamonds, emeralds, rubies, sapphires, pearls, and other precious stones; and the "gold from the teeth" and other gold deposits were to be handed over to the SS for "immediate delivery" to the Reichsbank in Berlin. The diamonds and other precious stones, which had to be appraised to determine their true value, would eventually be sent to KZ Vught in the Netherlands. The Nazis, with all their expertise and meticulousness in so many areas, had few Aryan professionals capable of doing the appraising, and in KZ Vught they had incarcerated the diamond merchants, cutters, and appraisers from Amsterdam and Antwerp, the experts who knew stones. Artistic implements—etching tools, paintbrushes, paints, magnifying lenses, and similar paraphernalia—were to be sent to KZ Sachsenhausen north of Berlin for the secret work being done there. Watches, timepieces of all kinds, pens, razors, pocketknives, scissors, flashlights, wallets, purses, and the like were to be sterilized, evaluated, and then delivered to the troops on the front lines. Every soldier was allowed to buy one watch, one knife, one razor, one flashlight, one pen, one pocketknife, with the proceeds going to the Reichsbank. Gold watches would be distributed among the SS. Men's underwear and shoes would be sorted, valued, and sold to ethnic Germans, as would women's and children's clothing, but not undergarments of silk, which were reserved for the Reich Ministry of Economics that distributed them to privileged Aryan women. Blankets, quilts, sheets, pillowcases, towels, tablecloths, table flatware, thermoses, combs, brushes, and the like were to be sold to ethnic Germans. Eyeglasses were destined for the Army Medical Corps, while gold frames were consigned to the SS. So, too, were furs.

The job of the children, under the watchful eyes of their SS guards, was to search the belongings of the dead or soon to be dead—their parents, their brothers and sisters, and other relatives. They examined the suitcases, the clothing, everything the detainees had brought with them, for hidden treasure, their fingers sliding along the hems and linings of garments to discover what might have been sewn into the folds, prying open the heels of shoes to see if they had been hollowed out to hold a gem, searching for secret compartments in the luggage, searching everywhere. Jack Eisner was fifteen when he was sent to Majdanek, and he spent the next year as one of those searchers.

In the middle of the warehouse were barrels, all marked with white letters designating their contents and their ultimate destinations—KZ Vught, KZ Sachsenhausen, Reichsbank, Finanzministerium, and more. Into one barrel went diamonds, cut and uncut; into others went rubies, sapphires, emeralds, precious stones of every description; into still others were tossed gold coins, silver coins, gold and silver goblets and candelabra, spectacles, and other valuables. And there were barrels for paintbrushes, etching and engraving tools, artists' implements of all kinds. Finally, there were the stacks of clothing and furs that had been gathered, sorted, heaped, tied into bundles—a barrel and a stack for everything.

Of particular and special interest to the SS masters of the warehouse were the Life Diamonds, those uncut stones gathered one or two at a time over the years by the wealthy Jews of Eastern Europe and then hidden in plain sight in seemingly innocuous, everyday household items. Somehow, someday, somewhere, the European Jews believed, those stones would buy freedom, prosperity, a new life. Now these uncut precious stones were hidden in secret compartments, in the hems and linings of clothing. They might have been missed in the past, but not at Majdanek, not when the methodical and avaricious eyes of the SS were watching so closely, eyes that missed nothing, hands that seized everything, even sugar cubes and toys.

The search by the children went on day after day for two weeks, as similar searches had been going on since the camp was established. Those two weeks, though, were a temporary reprieve from death, but only for those who worked without stopping, who never complained, who missed nothing. For anyone who complained, who was too slow to meet the SS's demands, whose hands were not quick enough or whose hands missed a treasure, who was so tired he nodded off, an SS bullet was the reward. Any of these infractions meant instant death. For the others, the reward was at least two weeks of life.

Some did survive, though only a few, through wits and an instinctive recognition that at least some of the Nazi guards were venal, were not above a little graft in exchange for protection. Swallow a diamond when no one was watching, retrieve it during the next bowel movement, pass it secretly to a willing guard, and the reward was a few extra days of life. Pass along a few diamonds and the guard might become a protector, hiding the child when the march to the showers began. Then repeat the process, the giving and protecting and hiding, as long as the flow of diamonds continued.

On a Sunday, Jack Eisner remembers, he was sitting about fifty feet from the camp fence when he noticed two Polish women walking cautiously on the outside. They were carrying two large loaves of bread. Approaching within fifteen feet of the electrified barbed-wire fence was forbidden, and could result in immediate death from the bullets of the guards in their watchtowers. Eisner hesitated, uncertain. The SS guard on the tower above just watched and grinned. The women began waving their arms at Eisner. "Come closer," they shouted. "Bread for diamonds or gold."

Eisner looked toward the SS guard. The guard grinned and nodded. Eisner took a deep breath and raced to the fence, pulled out two gold rings he had found during his search of the clothes in the warehouse, and passed them through the fence. The women took them and and passed him the bread and a slab of cheese, and then disappeared.

"It's nothing new," Eisner was told. "It goes on all the time. But make sure you pay the guard off. Just toss a package with some rings or gems over the fence. When the *yeke* goes off his shift, he'll pick it up and be happy." Eisner, though, was concerned with more than bread. He was concerned with survival. He hid diamonds, swallowing them, then going through his feces to retrieve them, repeating the process, and then slipping a diamond here and a diamond there to his guards. He buried diamonds in the ground near the fences when he could, informing the guards of their location so they could retrieve them, hoping that some would remain undiscovered so that, if he survived, as he was determined to do, he could dig them up when the war ended. (He never returned, however.) The SS guards came to cherish him for what he was giving them, and when the time came for the killing at the end of a fortnight, they would tell him to hide in the latrines until the selection was finished. He did. And he survived.

Indeed, it was no secret that camp personnel, all the way up to the commandants, embezzled gold and jewels for their own personal treasuries. Like Eisner, there were some children who survived by playing on the Nazis' greed. "In exchange for jewels or gold," remembers Joseph Uberkleider, one of whose jobs at Majdanek was to search the bodies of the dead as they were carried from the trains, "I succeeded in getting a piece of bread for myself, which is the reason I held out for a year in that hell. A new arrival once threw me a piece of soap and I had the luck to catch it. Soap was very precious, but this was even more precious. There was a diamond inside it. It bought me more bread."

The SS in Berlin, which proclaimed its purity and incorruptibility, did not look kindly on profiteering by its functionaries, no matter how highly placed; the plundered treasures of the Jews and others belonged not to one person but to the Reich. Both Commandants Koch and Florstedt, who had enriched themselves, were put on trial by the SS and sentenced to death.

Eisner was lucky, and so was Uberkleider. They got away with their ploys. Most didn't. For them, for almost all, there were the two weeks of labor and then, at the end, a forced march to the gas chambers. There was an endless stockpile of children to replace them. But before they died, they filled those barrels with valuable treasures.

Those barrels did not remain long at Majdanek or Birkenau or Sobibor or the other camps. Every Monday, convoys of trucks thundered out of the camps, rolling across the road made of broken tombstones from Jewish cemeteries that led from the crematoriums to the main gate, some loaded with clothing and canned goods for the troops at the front, others with shoes, dresses, undergarments of all kinds—anything someone might pay hard cash for and that the Nazis did not want—heading for the open markets of occupied Europe.

But the most important, those carrying the valuable loot amassed in those warehouses, departed in the dark, destined for shipment west. They passed the unloading docks where human cargo was being systematically herded from boxcars: one line destined for the barracks, where for a time, as long as energy lasted, as long as whim ruled, they would labor for the Reich, spend their days, until they could work no longer, as slaves for Krupp, or I. G. Farben, or Bayer, or some other German enterprise; the other line marched directly to the showers, to be bathed not with water but with Zyklon-B.

Those trucks moved on, through the gates in the electrified fences, passing the administration buildings, the barracks of the guards, the other structures, and then out and onto the highway.

The convoys sped through Poland and into Germany. Outside Berlin, some of the trucks veered off, headed into the city, toward the central treasury in a bunker two blocks behind the Reichskanzler. Another headed north, toward KZ Sachsenhausen, fifty-five miles from the city, with supplies for the very secret work in progress there.

And a third, with the most valuable cargo of all, the diamonds and other gems in the barrels marked KZ Vught, paused in Berlin, the glittering valuables within examined and relished by the Nazi overlords. Then that payload was supposed to race toward the Dutch border, its destination just outside the town of Hertogenbosch in the southern Netherlands—KZ Vught, the only designated concentration camp in Holland.

9

KZ Auschwitz II–Birkenau

Auschwitz wasn't big enough. Not big enough by far for the plans the Nazi hierarchy had for it. After the annexation of Polish Upper Silesia by the Third Reich, following the defeat of Poland, SS chief Heinrich Himmler ordered the construction of a concentration camp near the town of Oswiecim, thirty-seven miles west of Krakow, mainly to house Polish prisoners. The gates of Auschwitz swung open in late April 1940, and within a year more than eleven thousand prisoners, mainly Poles, were incarcerated there.

But by the spring of 1942, with the promulgation and implementation of *Akton Reinhard*, Auschwitz was designated for a new use. Here the Nazis would focus their energies on the eventual and total extermination of the European Jews in gas chambers and crematoriums. Here Jews would be used to ferret through the belongings of new arrivals and collect the hidden valuables, and here they would work until death as slave laborers for German corporations and for the camp personnel. As it stood then, the Auschwitz main camp was too small to accommodate such a wide-ranging series of tasks. And so, in March 1941, Himmler ordered the construction of a second and much larger camp in a birch forest across the railway line from the main camp at Auschwitz, a camp that could accommodate two hundred thousand prisoners, though none was expected to remain alive there for long. It was called KZ Auschwitz II–Birkenau. And it was labeled a *Vernichtungslager*—extermination camp.

Under the direction of Auschwitz's commandant, Rudolph Hess, it became just that. Somewhere between 2½ million and 4 million Jews, Poles, Gypsies, and Soviet prisoners of war were gassed in the seven gas chambers, each of which had the capacity to kill six thousand a day, and cremated in three crematoriums before the end of the war. The train station at Auschwitz II–Birkenau was the busiest in the world by 1944, the trains carrying sealed boxcars filled to capacity with men, women, and children arriving by the scores every day, unloading their human cargo, then departing empty to fetch another load and return.

And consider for a moment that human cargo. Unloaded at the Birkenau platform, they were forced to drop all their personal belongings by the side of the train, belongings that would be collected, searched meticulously by young Jewish inmates for valuables, and then bundled and crated for shipment west to the Reich. Then the arriving prisoners were herded in two lines, men in one, women and children in the other, past waiting SS examiners, who made the selections. The majority—the old, the infirm, and the very young—were marked for immediate gassing and cremation and forced to abandon all their garments. These clothes were heaped in piles to be searched by the young *Sonderkommando*. Then this group was marched to the "showers." The fit, the able, men and women and teenagers—all potential workers—were sent another way, to quarantine where they were stripped of their clothing and handed threadbare, striped prisoner uniforms, and the hair on their heads and bodies was shaved. They would become slaves of the Reich until they, too, were useless—beaten, tortured, starved until they could no longer work. Then they either died on the spot or followed the path to the chambers. None was expected to last more than a few months.

Pal Abraham was fifteen when he arrived at Birkenau with his family. His mother, father, sisters, grandparents, uncles, aunts, and cousins all perished there. Only he and a younger brother, who later died in Israel during the War for Independence, managed to survive. "I was in Block 5. Every evening we were put in one line and they checked us for lice. If they found one louse on you, that was your death. As soon as the sun came up, during the first weeks and months I was there, they marched us into the forest outside Sosnowiec to cut the trees. And the Germans would play games with us. One of them would go to someone and say, 'Go and get us some wood to build a fire,' and when he walked that way, they would shoot him in the back. We would go out in the morning fifty and come back four or five.

"Then I met a friend, Number 36 we called him. Those were some of the numbers tattooed on his arm. He told me that I was certain to die if I kept working in the forest. He said I should get transferred to the clothing if I wanted to survive. I managed that. What we did was sort out the clothing of the people who arrived on the transports. In everything, we always found something—gold and diamonds and other jewels. We would go through the clothes and other things and take what we found and put them in different barrels and crates, depending on what they were. And then the Nazis would take the treasures away when the barrels and crates were full. For food, they would give us soup and a piece of bread. What I would do was throw the bread in the soup at the beginning of the day and then, when nobody was looking, I would drop a diamond or another gem into the soup and it would stick to the bread so nobody could see it. At the end of the day, we were marched back to our barracks, and they had an orchestra playing happy marching songs as we marched, left, right, left, right, in a line, and if somebody didn't know his left from his right, they would throw him on the ground and beat him twenty-five times. As we marched through the gates, the guards would check us, examining everything to make sure that somebody hadn't tried to steal a diamond or some gold. But they never checked the plate in my hand because all they could see was the soup with a piece of bread floating in it. Those diamonds in the bread were what helped me to survive. They bought me bread and they bought me a potato or something else.

"Then they decided they had to build more crematoriums because they were killing people so fast. So they sent me there, and they sent me to collect the things from the dead. They sent me to pull out the gold teeth and take off the gold rings and search through the bodies to find a diamond that somebody might have hidden somewhere inside—the rectum, the mouth, the ears, the nose, between the toes, even the vaginas of the women. And what we found we had to put in those crates and barrels."

Dorit Klotz came from Romania. She was thirteen when she arrived at Birkenau in 1944. "They tattooed a number on my arm and they took us to work in this huge place near the crematorium. There was smoke coming out higher than the sky, and the smell of people burning. The smell has never left me. Our job was to collect the stuff from the people who came out of the trains and sort through it, and we did that ten hours a day every day. Every time a train with Jews arrived, we would sort things out and the boys would open the bags and the clothing and tear them apart. We would collect everything and tie them up in bundles of ten. But the money and the diamonds and the other treasures were different. Those we put in special barrels and crates, and at the end of the day trucks would come and take everything away.

"It was forbidden, but I managed to become friendly with some of the boys, the *Sonderkommando*. They had the worst job. They would have to take the dead bodies out of the gas chambers and then search those bodies, go through all the orifices, to find hidden treasures. At the end of three months as a *Sonderkommando*, the boys would be thrown into the gas chambers and the crematoriums themselves and then new boys would replace them. On Succoth, some of us decided to try to save some of these boys who were going to be killed. We started fires in our barracks so that the SS would rush our way and try to put out the fires and then some of the boys could escape, or because guns had been smuggled to them, at least kill some of the SS. We got the fires going and then we heard the SS running around and screaming and beating people, and then I heard Jewish singing and then shooting outside the crematoriums. Something had gone wrong. Someone had told the SS our plans and the SS were ready and they killed the boys right there, but the boys died singing, and they even managed to kill some of the SS, which got the SS even angrier. We didn't save them, but at least we tried."

Every day the trucks rolled west from Auschwitz II–Birkenau to enrich the coffers of the Third Reich. When Soviet troops finally liberated Auschwitz on January 27, 1945, the SS had abandoned the camp so hastily that some of the spoils remained, yet to be sent to the Reich. They included 836,525 items of women's clothing, 348,820 items of men's clothing, 43,525 pairs of shoes, seven tons of human hair, and an uncounted number of eyeglasses, toothbrushes, and other personal effects. But no gold and no diamonds. Even in the panic that overcame the SS in the final moments, they left none of that treasure behind.

10

KZ Vught

This was a special place, from the moment it was erected near the city of Hertogenbosch, nineteen miles northwest of Eindhoven in the southern Netherlands, on January 13, 1943. It was named officially *Konzentrationslager Herzogenbosch,* but called KZ Vught by those who ruled there and those who were brought there as prisoners. It was the only officially designated concentration camp in the Netherlands, and is today only a vague memory, called by scholars one of the "forgotten camps." The absolute ruler was Commandant Karl Chmielewski, sent to Vught from the Gusen subcamp of Mauthausen where he had earned a reputation for extreme brutality. He brought with him eighty Kapos who knew how to deal with prisoners, and a battalion of SS troops, officers and enlisted men, who would be exclusively in charge of all aspects of Vught. Barracks were hastily erected to house the expected influx of prisoners, a gallows constructed to hang some, a crematorium set in place to dispose of the bodies, and, a half-mile from the camp, a killing center established, called *De Ijzeren Man,* the Iron Man, to which those marked to die were marched, lined up, and then shot by firing squads.

Three days after Vught's establishment, the first of the prisoners arrived. Among them was a group that would play a major role in KZ Vught's future. They were some of the Jewish diamond experts from Amsterdam, Antwerp, and the other diamond centers in the Low Countries. They were placed in barracks in the *Schutzhaftlager,* the Security Camp.

A second section of Vught, and the most populated, was called the *Judendurchgangslager,* the transit camp for Jews. And a transit camp it was. The new arrivals would be at Vught only temporarily, they were told, before going on to a more permanent camp, at *Centraal Vluchtalinger Kamp Westerbork,* the Central Refugee Camp at Westerbork. But Westerbork, they discovered once there, was anything but a permanent home. It was just another way station for the Jews of the Low Countries, a *Durchgangslager,* a transit camp, the central clearinghouse for *Entjudung*—the cleansing of the Netherlands and Belgium of the Jews. From Westerbork, they were shipped to Auschwitz II–Birkenau and to Sobibor, to the extermination centers in Poland. It was this route, this road to death—Vught to Westerbork to the East—that was the path of those like Anne Frank and her family after their capture in the secret annex, the attic shelter in Amsterdam.

But for a time the fate of those in the security camp, even if death ultimately lay at the end, was different. This section was reserved for political prisoners and forced laborers, though the lot of at least some of the laborers was considerably better than in nearly every other concentration camp. The privilege, if it could be called that, of using Vught's prisoners as workers was handed to Philips Electronics, N.V., one of the most important companies in Holland. It was not a gift the company welcomed, any more than it welcomed the occupation of its country by the Germans. Throughout a Europe controlled by the Nazis, many of the largest and most important industrial corporations eagerly sought and accepted slave laborers and filled their coffers with the profits they made from this free source of labor, concerned not at all with the consequences of working those "slaves" to death.

Philips was a notable exception. The company's president, F. J. (Frits) Philips, and major executives did not buy into the Nazi philosophy regarding Jews. The safety, and rescue, of Philips' Jewish employees became a major concern as the Nazi tide rolled over Europe. At its Austrian subsidiary, all the Jewish workers were sheltered, declared essential to the war effort, and all survived under Philips' protection. At its subsidiary in Lithuania, Philips executives provided visas to Curaçao for Polish and Baltic Jews in its employ. This despite regulations promulgated by the Nazi regime in Holland forbidding Dutch-based companies from aiding Jews in any manner, Philips managed to rescue nearly five thousand.

The efforts of Philips' executives to protect its Jewish employees throughout Europe, indeed, even Jews who were not employees, were matched back in the Netherlands. Until the spring of 1941, there seemed no need to take special steps to shelter Philips' Jews from the Nazis. All that changed that spring as the Nazis tightened their grip.

Matters grew worse in the fall of 1941, when the Nazis issued decrees informing Dutch companies that they could—or should—dismiss their Jewish workers. Philips directors and Jewish staff members met and decided to set up a Special Development Bureau, called Sobu, into which all Jewish employees would be transferred, in the hope that German authorities would then leave the Jews, and Philips, alone. It was a vain hope. The Nazis quickly restricted the freedom of movement the Sobu members had enjoyed, and then forced Philips to reduce their wages. That was just the start. While Sobu continued to enjoy some protection, it did not extend to their families and Jewish friends. All over Holland, they were being fired, forced from their homes, their possessions seized. "No day went by," wrote a Philips executive, "without somebody losing someone dear to them. Here a brother was taken, there a father, there a brother-in-law."

In order to forestall German moves against its Jewish employees, Philips moved them all to Eindhoven and began to explore the possibility of obtaining exit visas for them. In August 1942, Frits Philips sent a message to the United States. "Now I have one request, and that is that America should at least make available the equivalent of two million guilders to save the lives of Jews in the company by obtaining exit visas from the occupied territories—which is sometimes possible. I do not think that with goodwill there should be no means of finding a solution to this."

It was late in the day, unfortunately, for such a plan to work. The United States was at war with Germany by then and was not about to let dollars, or guilders, flow into the Nazi coffers. And then, on November 24, the German-dominated government in The Hague announced that buying the freedom of Dutch Jews with foreign currency was forbidden.

If that plan was dead, another was put forward. The head of Philips' travel office had made important contacts with influential Germans who told him they would cooperate in facilitating the emigration of Sobu members and their families, along with some other Amsterdam Jews. In return, the Germans would want to attach a few German Jews to the group to act as spies. It worked. Between May 1941 and January 1942, 486 Dutch Jews escaped from the occupation via Spain to North and South America.

This looked like the beginning of a mass exodus. Extensive negotiations between Philips and the Spanish led to the promise that enough transit visas for another three hundred Jews would be issued to take care of all who wanted to travel, as long as the group left Spain promptly. Haste was essential because, as one Philips executive wrote, "Staying in Holland means for the greater part death." At Eindhoven and in Amsterdam, the would-be travelers began packing frantically. Labels for suitcases were printed, seats were being allocated on the trains, buses, and ships. The only question asked by many was, Where are we going?

And then the planned escape collapsed. On June 30, 1943, the Germans announced that the plan was *kaput*. Sobu members and their families and other Jews would be sent not to safety but to the transit camp at Westerbork or to KZ Vught.

If they were sent to Vught, the thought of many was, there at least they would still be under the protection of Philips. In the Philips workshops at Vught, the company employed 1,200 prisoners, called the *Philipskommando,* and insisted that its Jewish workers—even those who had not been on the payroll in peacetime—have decent working conditions, a hot meal every day, and medical treatment, and that anyone Philips was using must not be subject to deportation to the extermination camps in the East. The company also demanded that its workers be paid. That demand was met for only a few weeks, and then the SS rulers of Vught banned the payment of wages in cash, said that from that moment on, payment would be in the form of camp coupons that could be used in the "camp shop," a place with mainly bare shelves.

But, as the war was nearing its end and Canadian, Scottish, and British troops were closing in on the Netherlands, even the protected Philips workers were sent east, to Auschwitz. Once there, Philips still tried its best to save them, striking an agreement with the German electronics company, Telefunken, one of those not above taking advantage of slaves for profit. The agreement called for Philips' workers to receive preferential treatment. That agreement, though, did not last. In the final stages of the war, the slaughter of the Jews at Auschwitz II–Birkenau encompassed Philips' Dutch laborers. Only 160 of the 517 people in the Philips pool who reached Auschwitz survived the war, two-thirds of the women and nine children.

And then there were those in the special barracks, those with special talents that the Nazis wanted to use—the diamond merchants, appraisers, cutters, specialists in the world of precious stones—about two hundred of them in all. It was to them that the diamonds from Majdanek, Birkenau, and the other camps in the East were destined, as were the diamonds stolen from the jewelry centers in Amsterdam and Antwerp. There they were to be examined and appraised, some cut, and then turned over to the Nazi warlords in Berlin, to Himmler and the others in the hierarchy. As the war neared its end, as Germany's defeat became inevitable, the best were hidden and clandestinely passed on to SS officers at Vught for their own private benefit, and possible salvation. With all those diamonds and all the other looted treasures, the Nazis who managed to escape would have all the means they needed to pay for protection wherever they settled, and enough to live the good life for the rest of their days.

The diamond experts from Amsterdam and Antwerp waited for the diamonds, waited to work on them. It was what they had been told they were at Vught for, why they had been spared the fate of most Jews caught in the Nazi noose. This was their assigned task, to work for the benefit of the Reich or, rather, for their own survival. It had haunted them since the arrival in Holland of the German army.

"When the Germans came to Holland," remembers Jacques Furth, now in his nineties and one of the few survivors of KZ Vught, "there were many of us who worked in the diamond business who were afraid. We knew and we heard what they did in other places. But at first with us it was different. The Germans did not send the SS or the Gestapo to look for us. No, they sent Dutch collaborators who went from one workshop to the others, to all the people in the industry, telling us not to worry, that trouble was not coming to us but that we were all going to be working like before. These Dutch collaborators told us that the Germans needed the diamond industry and that we who worked in the cutting and polishing and other parts of the industry were very important to the Germans. We believed them because we wanted to believe them, because they were like us, Dutch and not German.

"Then they asked the storeowners and the workshop owners to give them lists of every stone they had, the cut ones and the polished ones and the uncut ones, the size and the price. We all thought this was a good sign and that maybe they were changing the way they did things so it would not be bad for us. They told us not to hide things, because everything would be fine for us.

"Two weeks later, when we were back at work, we knew life was not normal, but it was not like we were in hell. Then they came in the middle of the day, all at once, to every shop and every workplace and they took everything, every diamond, every precious stone. They came and took it all, and there were at least eight hundred stores, workshops, and little factories in Holland, and they came to them all and took everything. Then they did something very clever. They came back and left us with the very cheap and very small stones and told us that we were still going to be doing work, but not as much as before.

"They stole everything and then left us with just enough diamonds to show their masters back in Berlin that everything was still working. The SS were the biggest thieves. I think they had it all planned out. They took what they could and they wanted the people back home in Germany to think the diamond industry was still working, but now not for Holland but for Hitler. That is why they left us alone with the small, cheap stones for almost a year.

"And then they came back, in September 1943, and they took us all to the camp. That was when they had stopped lying to the world. That was when they did not need to keep up the front; it did not matter anymore. So they sent us to Vught, and there we waited for many months. Some of us were put on transports and others, sent to work camps. But all the time they kept the diamond people together. I did not understand why; there were no diamonds for most of us to work on. But they kept us separate from the others, as if they had something special planned for us.

"Then I was called to the commandant of the camp. I was not the most experienced worker there, but I was well known, for I had started some workshops in Amsterdam. The commandant told me to take some men, and he sent us back to Amsterdam, and he tells us to bring back to the camp what we had left behind in the workplaces, the biggest and the most modern machines we could find. He sent soldiers with us, and they put the machines, which were very dirty because they had not been used in a long time, on trucks and took them back to Vught. And there was a special building for us in the corner of the camp. It was apart from the rest. When we had the machines in the building, the commandant said he wanted them all cleaned and painted like new, and we did that, and we got everything to work, and it all looked new.

"Then I understood. This German wanted me to sign a paper saying that I have put in new machines, so he could get money for doing that, for buying new equipment. And then we waited, and we waited in that special factory we had built for the diamond industry. But nothing happened. We didn't work because the Germans did not send any raw diamonds for us to work on. Those thieves, after they had stolen the diamonds, they did not trust each other, and they were not going to send anything they already had their hands on back to Holland. We in our new factory were not going to get any diamonds. It was all a show for Berlin.

"And then they sent us to the extermination camps when we were no longer needed."

That sham diamond factory didn't remain at Vught either. It was dismantled, packed up, and sent to Bergen Belsen.

Jacques Furth is convinced that the letters on the pouch that Sam Nyer and his fellow U.S. Army Scout Tommy DeLion liberated from the SS were *KZ Vught*. He is also certain that the diamonds in it—those rough, uncut diamonds stolen from the stocks in Amsterdam and Antwerp, and from the Jews in the death camps—were supposed to be on their way from Berlin to his diamond factory at Vught, or at least that's what the Nazi hierarchy was led to believe. The thieves in the SS, as he calls them, had no intention of letting them travel that far. They diverted them to their own private caches in Strasbourg or one of the nearby towns.

While Jacques Furth and the people with him waited in vain in their isolated sham factory, diamonds were actually arriving at KZ Vught without his knowledge. They were arriving in trucks and specially armored staff cars, from the East (both the occupied East—the death camps—and the closer East, Berlin, where the diamonds from the death camps had initially been brought, and where diamonds stolen in Amsterdam and Antwerp had first been sent). The diamonds were carried to secret, curtained-off areas in the barracks. Under the watchful eyes of an SS officer, the specialists appraised and divided them. Cut stones went here, uncut stones went there; perfect stones here, flawed ones there; the most valuable in one place, the less valuable in another. This was no simple job. It required a perfect eye and understanding of the gems, for there are fourteen thousand categories of diamonds based on combinations of size, shape, color, and clarity, and the value depended on the quality. (Today, the best diamonds sell for more than $25,000 a carat.)

The chief appraiser, prized above all others by his SS masters, was a young Jew in his mid-twenties who would later adopt the identity and name of a dead Jew named Lieb Zuckerman. Not Zuckerman then, but using his family name, he arrived at Vught in early 1944. He was born into a semireligious, German-Jewish, diamond-merchant family in Upper Silesia, a family with a strict and unbending moral view of the world. At an early age, he became an object of opprobrium in his family. Though he showed a talent for the diamond business, it was his personal life that brought him into disfavor. He was a homosexual. He would have to be dispatched elsewhere to be reeducated and reindoctrinated if the family's reputation were to remain unblemished. He was sent to friends in Antwerp in the mid-1930s as an apprentice diamond cutter. He learned cutting, and more important, he had an eye for value, for appraising, which, despite his youth and despite his sexual leanings, made him a very valuable asset to the firm.

In the spring of 1940, he and a Dutch homosexual lover with whom he had established a lengthy relationship moved to Amsterdam. He signed on with a prestigious firm as its major appraiser. Two weeks later, on May 15, 1940, the Nazis marched in, and the Netherlands capitulated. Appointed to rule the newly occupied nation was the notorious Austrian Nazi, Arthur Seyss-Inquart, named *der Reichskommissioner für die besetzten niederländischen Gebiete* and responsible only to Adolf Hitler himself. Though Seyss-Inquart promised the Dutch in a formal speech that Germany had no intention of annexing the nation nor forcing its policies down the throats of the Dutch, that promise was like all Nazi promises. Within weeks, the Nazi ideology was in full force. Jews, who had been considered Dutch citizens, who had all the rights of other Dutchmen, were now stripped of those rights, forced to register, forced to wear the yellow star, enlisted into forced labor details in Holland, and dispatched to Germany itself.

Zuckerman was no exception. Like everyone else, he was forced to register. But for him there was a dilemma. He was a German national living in Holland. He was also a Jew, and a homosexual. If it was possible to have three strikes against you at the start, he was saddled with those three strikes. Jews had been stripped of their German citizenship by Nazi law, but were subject to the whim of the Reich's rulers. Jews and homosexuals were considered subhuman and marked for extermination. If Zuckerman registered as a German national and as a Jew and as a homosexual, he knew he would be shipped out on the first transport to the East to whatever fate lay in store for him there. "But for some reason," he says, "they gave me a choice. They ignored the fact that I was born in Germany and put me down as Dutch. And even though I had a Jewish name, they told me I could be registered as a Jew or as a homosexual. I didn't have to register as both. I knew what the Nazis were doing to the Jews, and maybe they weren't quite so anxious to get rid of homosexuals, so I chose homosexual, and they put that down and they gave me the pink triangle."

After registering, he went back to work for his employers, as had Jacques Furth and other diamond specialists. But that lasted only until late 1942, when the Nazis tightened their grip on the Netherlands. He was seized in a roundup and sent to the Amersfoort detention camp, remained there for a time, then was sent to the detention camp at Eindhoven, and then to Westerbork, slated for transportation to the killing centers in the East. Before he could be sealed in a boxcar, though, someone examined his records, saw his background, and realized that he was more valuable to the Reich alive than dead. The next thing he knew, he was at KZ Vught.

There were eighty-seven inmates in his barracks, sleeping on narrow bunks piled one on top of the other, floor to ceiling, almost all assigned to work for Philips during the day, and, like Jacques Furth, waiting to work on the diamonds that were never given to them. He was the exception. Diamonds were his only task. Zuckerman was assigned his own space, a tiny, curtained-off cubicle at the rear of the barracks containing not merely a single cot, but a small wood-burning stove. In the cubicle, too, on a raised platform, was an old printer's table, a flat surface behind which were rows of pigeonholes; once a printer had slotted his fonts in those holes. Now they were used for the sorting of gems.

When a new shipment arrived from Berlin, it was divided up, with part assigned to his counterpart in one barracks, part to the appraiser in the other, the rest to the man who would, on a train to the East in 1945, become Lieb Zuckerman. One day the shipment would be gold watches and other gold jewelry, even gold fillings ripped from the mouths of the dead; another day, rubies or emeralds or sapphires or pearls.

Most important of all, though, were the diamonds, the cut stones and the rough, uncut ones, the Life Diamonds. With an SS officer standing over him, watching carefully, Zuckerman would adjust the loupe over his eye and carefully examine the stones, appraising them, almost always and unfailingly able to tell after a brief study the quality and value of the gems. When necessary, when uncertain, he would cut a small window in an uncut diamond to gain a better perspective. When he was certain, the stones before him would be placed in those pigeonholes, gem-quality stones in one hole, lesser-quality cut stones in others, best-quality uncut stones in yet another. The slots were marked, *A* for the best, *B, C,* and *D* for lesser ones. Then the divided diamonds would be gathered by grade and placed in purple leather pouches stamped *KZ Vught* and readied for another journey back to the East. This time they were headed for the Fatherland, for the enrichment of the Third Reich, which would now be certain of the value of the stones that it had plundered.

By mid-1944, there was a change in the operation. After the Allied landings on Normandy and on the Mediterranean coast of France, and with the rapid Allied advances, Germany's defeat was imminent, and the SS at Vught and elsewhere grew increasingly concerned about their own futures. New orders were given to Zuckerman and the other appraisers. The diamonds and other jewels marked *B, C,* and *D* were still to be placed in those purple leather pouches and carried to Berlin. For the gems marked *A,* the best, there was another destination.

In the occupied countries of the West, especially France, the SS and the Wehrmacht, the German Army, had freedoms that did not exist in the Fatherland. At home, the rule of the Nazi overlords was rigid and unbending. Meticulous records were kept of all the treasures received—what they were and how many, whence they came, where they were heading, who would receive them. Everything was entered into ledgers and the treasures were audited on a continuing basis. Not so once the borders into the occupied nations were crossed. Those territories were ruled by the SS and the Wehrmacht, and they made their own rules, unhampered by the strictures at home. And so in Strasbourg and nearby towns along the Rhine River, especially, the SS and the Wehrmacht established a network of private depositories. To those depositories went the best, the most valuable. When the war ended, when Germany lay at the mercy of the victorious Allies, its leaders dead or imprisoned, those who had ruled and terrorized the occupied nations had no intention of sharing similar fates if they could help it. They were determined to have the means, the wealth, to vanish and start a new existence somewhere beyond the victors' reach. If doing so meant violating the precepts of National Socialism, so be it. When the choice had to be made between philosophy and self-interest, self-interest—survival—would inevitably win out.

This Zuckerman knew very well. He was a case in point. Under the laws of the Reich, Jews and homosexuals were subhuman species not to be tolerated, to be exterminated as quickly as possible. Zuckerman was a Jew. Zuckerman was a practicing homosexual. Yet Zuckerman was not only *not* exterminated, not merely tolerated, but protected, guarded, entrusted with the fortunes and the futures of those who thought themselves his masters.

So he did their bidding. He appraised the stones, pouched them as he was directed, turned the *B, C,* and *D* pouches over to the Reich's couriers to be carried to Berlin, and turned the *A* pouches over to his SS guardians for their own use. But he protected himself in case he fell into disfavor. He told them he was keeping a list of all the stones he graded and to whom he gave them. He told them he was not merely keeping that list, but somehow managing to smuggle it out of Vught to a farmer who passed the camp every morning. If Zuckerman did not appear one morning, or if the farmer heard that something had happened to Zuckerman, the farmer had instructions to send the list immediately to Gestapo headquarters in Berlin. If that happened, Zuckerman told his SS keepers, they would soon find themselves and their families hanging from lampposts in their hometowns with signs around their necks proclaiming that they had stolen from the Third Reich.

"It was nonsense, just a story I made up," he says. "How could I have smuggled such a list out of the camp, and what farmer would have done what I asked? But it didn't matter. They believed me, or they were afraid not to believe me. They were terrified that their Nazi superiors back home would learn what they were doing and do to them what they were doing to us, to all the Jews."

It worked. Until early September 1944, when he suddenly found himself on a train bound for KZ Sachsenhausen, he labored, appraised, and sorted the diamonds and other gems under the eyes of his SS watchdog with little fear.

By the time the Fourth Canadian Armored Division and the 96th Battery of the Canadian Fifth Anti-Tank Division marched into KZ Vught on October 27, 1944, Zuckerman was gone, and so were most of the Jews (twelve thousand had been in Vught) and even the non-Jewish diamond people. This was the beginning of the long and tortuous liberation of the Netherlands that would last until spring—Holland was the last country in occupied Europe to be freed, having suffered longer under the Nazi heel that any other nation except Norway. Inside the camp they found five hundred bodies, prisoners who had been executed by the SS that morning. Another five hundred to six hundred remained barely alive, and only had a chance to survive because of the arrival of the Canadians. They had been scheduled for execution that afternoon. As the SS fought a last desperate battle with the Canadians, those prisoners, traumatized by their ordeal, merely stood in the camp's courtyard waiting, not seeking shelter, saved only by the Canadian victory. They were the lucky ones, not merely in Vught but of all the Jews in Holland. Before the war there had been 140,000 Jews in the country. When the liberation came, only 35,000 remained alive. The percentage of Jews slaughtered in the Netherlands was the highest of any country outside Poland.

And before the war, the Netherlands had been about the richest and most prosperous country in Europe. At the end of the war, as a result of Nazi acts of devastation, it was one of the poorest.

Today, Vught still exists, not as a prison camp but as a national prison where hundreds of convicted felons are incarcerated. The memory of what transpired there half a century ago, though, is preserved in one corner of the prison yard. In April 1990, Queen Beatrix dedicated the National Monument Camp Vught on that small plot of ground. Preserved there are some of the relics of those terrible times—two huge ovens in the brick crematorium, and much more—and some reconstructions, such as a barracks complete with wooden cots and a brick torture room about the size of an automobile. A fifteen-minute walk from the prison into the woods, the Iron Man still stands.

On a dark overcast afternoon in early September 1944, Zuckerman, as he had been doing since his arrival at KZ Vught, finished a day sorting and appraising his stack of diamonds, dividing them according to quality and value. When he completed that task, he sat back and stared at the treasures in the pigeonholes at the back of his desk. He reached out and gathered forty of the most valuable Life Diamonds, placed them in one of those purple leather pouches stamped *KZ Vught*, and handed the pouch to an SS officer who stood over him, watching and waiting. The SS officer took the pouch and placed it securely in a briefcase he locked with a chain around his wrist. Without a word or gesture to Zuckerman, he spun around and strode from the workroom, from the barracks, out to a waiting Wehrmacht staff car with a special traveling insignia. Behind the staff car was a BMW motorbike, machine gun mounted on the sidecar. Another BMW motorbike with a mounted machine gun was in front of the car. The SS officer climbed into the rear of the car.

Zuckerman watched him go. He had watched similar scenes, similar departures throughout his time at KZ Vught. It was a pattern he had grown used to. He was sure he knew just where those forty diamonds were going. He was sure he knew just what their future would be. He was sure he knew whom they would enrich. He was sure it would not be the Reich hierarchy, not Hitler and Himmler and the others in Berlin.

Outside the barracks he heard the car's engine turn over. He walked to the entrance and watched the small caravan move out of KZ Vught into the gathering dusk of that September afternoon. It began a journey that was supposed to take it to Berlin, to the waiting Nazi overlords.

It never reached Berlin. Instead, as it neared the Rhine crossing, it turned south and then west, heading toward Strasbourg or one of the nearby towns.

But the journey of the diamonds, forty of the uncut, rough ones at least, was not over. Ahead lay Sam Nyer and, after him, Yaron Svoray.

PART II

Sam Nyer's Journey

11

A World at War

On the night he and Svoray met in Bangor, Sam Nyer began his story, and Svoray made the time to hear him out. He listened through that night, first in the lecture hall, then at a nearby diner, and finally in the Nyers's living room. Svoray listened for eight hours, stayed on in Bangor, and listened again for hours more, and he kept returning and listening for more nights in the years to come, constantly marveling at Nyer's memory. It seemed the man remembered the tiniest detail from forty years earlier—remembered conversations, attitudes, everything—and had an answer to the scores of questions Svoray asked. Svoray kept probing more deeply with the encouragement of his wife, Mikhal, who thought perhaps he had stumbled onto a good story that might lead to something profitable. Svoray enveloped himself in Nyer's tale, in what he soon realized was Nyer's obsession.

The long and rambling saga begun that first night led inexorably to two crucial episodes. The first occurred early in January 1945; the second, about seven weeks later, on February 26, 1945, though the year that preceded those dates, indeed, all that went before, was a necessary prelude to them, and to what followed.

Nyer had been an advance scout in a company of the U.S.

Seventh Army commanded by Major General Alexander Patch, who had led the final assault that defeated the Japanese on Guadalcanal in 1943 before being reassigned to the European theater and to his new command. Sam Nyer had been a scout since shipping out to Europe in the fall of 1944, though how he got to be a scout was always something of a mystery to him. He had enlisted in the Army before finishing his first year at an agricultural college in Pennsylvania, after being rejected by both the Marines and the Navy because he was color-blind. "My father sent me to that college, even though I was a city kid living in Brooklyn, because I was always interested in farming, but more important, because he wanted to keep me out of the war. But I got tired of college and I was reading the newspapers and I felt I should get into the thing as every good American kid was trying to do. I thought it was especially important for a Jewish kid because of what we heard the Nazis were doing to the Jews. I was eighteen, and I'd have been drafted in another few months anyway, so I just got a jump on things. At that time, all the movies and stories didn't have anything about what war was really like. They made it look like war was just full of glory and bravery and things like that. I had no idea what was really what. So I enlisted. I figured I'd have some choice if I did that rather than wait."

Nyer did basic training at Fort Bragg, North Carolina, where he turned down an opportunity to go to officer candidate school. "I'd been training to be in the artillery for about two months when they made me that offer. I said, 'If I go to OCS, what branch of the service will I be a lieutenant in?' They said, 'The infantry.'

"I said, 'No, thanks, I'll stay a private in the artillery.' I knew that they wanted to turn me into what they called in those days a ninety-day wonder and then ship me out to an infantry unit as a replacement for another ninety-day wonder, and the result would have been that in about a week I'd be on my way home in a box. I knew by then that what the movies showed had nothing to do with reality, and I was learning what really happened to guys in the infantry. You know, one, two, three, and that was it. I figured if I stayed a private in the artillery, I'd have a lot better chance to stay alive."

He ended up in the infantry anyway, as a private instead of an officer. His battalion was converted from artillery into an infantry unit and sent to Fort Jackson in South Carolina for six weeks' training and then overseas as replacements. "Somebody must have figured as long as I was in the infantry, and I'd refused the chance to be an officer, they'd give me the worst detail they had, the one with the least chance of survival. So they said, 'Sam, you're a scout.'

"I said, 'What's a scout?'

"They said a scout was a guy who went out in front of everybody to find the best way to get someplace and then reported back. A scout was a guy who collected intelligence while everybody else waited behind.

"I said, 'You mean, I go out all by my lonesome while all the other guys stay nice and safe?'

"They said, 'No, you have a partner with you.'

"I said, 'You mean, just the two of us and that's it?'

"They said, 'That's the way it is.'"

On the boat overseas, sailing through the South Atlantic to avoid the German submarine wolf packs that infested the North Atlantic sea-lanes, Sam Nyer practiced the techniques of a scout. He learned how to use a knife, learned how to use a garrote (a metal wire attached to two sticks, a silent killing machine), learned how to move without a sound, surreptitiously, learned how to to stay alive.

On August 15, 1944, the Seventh Army, which had been in combat in Italy, was relieved of its Italian duties and, with the

French First Army at its side, struck at what Winston Churchill called the soft underbelly of Europe in Operation Anvil-Dragoon, landing between Nice and Marseilles on the Mediterranean coast of France. The Americans and the French moved rapidly north, their aim to split and trap the German forces and link up with American and British armies advancing east from the breakouts in Normandy and Brittany.

In early November, Nyer's unit linked up with the Seventh Army in Vosges. Day after day, Sam Nyer and a partner moved out ahead, usually after dark, to scout the terrain, to gather intelligence. And day after day, he wondered if this would be his last day. The average life expectancy of a scout was measured in minutes, or, at best, hours. But somehow Sam Nyer survived with barely a scratch. His partners were not so lucky. One after another they fell to German snipers and land mines, only to be immediately replaced, some falling so quickly that he barely had time to learn their names.

Through the summer and early fall of 1944, the Seventh Army and its French allies, commanded by General Jean de Lattre de Tassigny, drove steadily up the Rhone Valley. They liberated Lyon on September 3, and by autumn reached the Vosges Mountains, a 120-mile chain covered by dense, wild pine forests extending from the Lorraine plateau in the west to the Alsatian plain. About then, Nyer's unit was detached from the Seventh Army at that point and attached to the First French Army. German resistance stiffened as the temperatures plummeted, the beginning of one of the worst winters in forty years.

"In the mountains," Sam Nyer remembers, "it was below zero, and the snow was up to your knees, and the fighting was hand to hand. We kept sending out probes, scouts like me and my partners, behind German lines, and they kept sending out probes behind our lines, and we started losing a lot of men, and so did they. It was when we reached the mountains that I lost this guy who was with me; he must have been maybe the third or fourth partner I'd lost. This guy was from West Virginia, a real hillbilly. He became my friend, which happened only after a while, after one freezing night when it was so cold we were sitting in a foxhole, and he was sitting between my knees and we were hugging each other so we could keep warm. We start talking and he says, 'You know who caused this war? The Jews.'

"He'd never seen a Jew in his life and he was talking like that. I listened to him for a while and he says, 'You would never find a Jew on the front lines, never.' I took out my knife and I stabbed him a half-inch into his back, and he jumped up screaming, 'What happened?'

"I said, 'You just found a Jew on the front lines.' We became good buddies after that, only pretty soon he got killed."

His replacement was a little guy, about five-feet-four, with a dark complexion, as though he had spent most of his life in the sun. He was an American Indian named Tommy DeLion, though Nyer was not sure how he spelled it. "I don't think he even knew how himself. I mean, Tommy could barely read a word, he was next thing to illiterate. And he had this kind of accent. He couldn't even pronounce my name right. He used to call me Sum."

Tommy DeLion was not supposed to have been a scout. Nyer was sure he was supposed to have been in the Signal Corps as a radio operator, the usual job assigned to Indians. The Army was convinced that nobody but another Indian could understand their languages, and so the Germans would never be able to decipher radio messages relayed from one Indian to another in their native tongues. But Tommy could never figure out just how to operate a radio, just as he could barely speak English, so the Army gave up and sent him to the front as a scout. It was a wise decision. Together, Sam Nyer and Tommy DeLion won chests full of medals, including for each three Bronze Stars, Purple Hearts, and more, and managed to dodge every danger in the process. "We became friends immediately. My life depended on him; and his, on me. I figured it was the combination of Tommy's hunting and trekking skills and my photographic memory and street smarts that made us such a good team. The only thing about Tommy was he smoked like a chimney. I mean, he smoked all day and all night. The only benefit was that maybe we got a little heat in our foxhole. Other than that, it was smoke, and we would choke all night, and sometimes I'd get out of the foxhole and lie on the ground and he'd be in there choking himself to death. I'd say, 'Tommy, what are you doing that for?'

"And he'd say, 'I'm nervous,' which was a good answer."

The winter war in the Vosges Mountains was particularly brutal for the GIs whose only shelter against the elements was to burrow into shallow foxholes.

"At that time, and I'd say for most of the war, my part in it, we lived like animals. As a matter of fact, animals lived better. We were constantly agitated, constantly under enemy fire. There was no sleep. The food was rotten, and I don't mean just terrible, I mean it was rotten all the way through. They could hardly get food up to us. One day a can of chicken and rice appeared and me and another guy grabbed for it, and he's holding the can and I'm reaching for it and we're tugging at it, and I said, 'I saw it. It's my can,' and he says, 'It's my can,' and we started pushing each other, and he took out his knife and I took out my knife, and we were going to start fighting with knives until the sergeant broke it up. All this over one lousy can of chicken and rice.

"We all got viruses, things you couldn't imagine; everybody was throwing up all the time. It was so cold my feet froze. I didn't have gloves. I didn't have boots, just my old combat boots with the leather worn thin. We were going six or seven weeks without any day relief—no baths, no toothpaste, no shaves. We wore the same clothes for weeks—the same socks, the same everything, no change—and after a while we were crawling with maggots and we were filthy, dirty, smelled like excrement. I was 150 pounds when I went into the Army and during that time I lost 30 of those pounds.

In the mountains, they were constantly on edge, always in some kind of battle or skirmish, and they had no idea what was going on anywhere else. They didn't know what was happening a hundred feet down the line, and they didn't have a clue about what was going on at home or even anywhere else in the war. They got *Stars and Stripes* every two or three days, so everything they learned was from the military's perspective. At that point, they knew nothing about the Holocaust or what was happening to the Jews, though there were lots of rumors and, of course, there were all the stories that had been spread widely before the war. But they never heard the word *Holocaust* until the war was over.

"At first, I didn't hate the Germans, not until I started to hear the rumors about what they were doing to the Jews, and not until I started to see what they did to some of our guys who were captured. We would pick up men as we advanced who had been torn apart, but at first we didn't know how, and then we found out they had been prisoners and were killed. That's when I really started to hate the Germans.

"One time during a daylight attack, we were attacking the Germans and they were attacking us at the same time, and we were getting artillery fire from both sides and machine-gun fire from both sides, and men were dropping like flies. We started retreating, and the Germans started retreating, and I jumped into a hole in the ground about two or three hundred feet from our line and the same distance away from the Germans. It started to get dark and I jumped into this foxhole to escape the artillery fire. I had a bayonet on the end of my rifle and I left it sticking up in case anyone jumped into this foxhole with me. Unfortunately, our bayonets couldn't cope with anything, you couldn't even open a can of beans with them.

"All of a sudden a body landed on top of my bayonet. I pushed the body to the opposite side of the foxhole. In what light there was I could see he was a German officer and the bayonet had hardly injured him, just a few bruises. I said, '*Hani hop,*' you know, German for raise your hands. He didn't. I said it again, and he started talking to me in English. His hands were still down and he started reaching into his coat. I jabbed him with the bayonet and reached in and he had a pistol, which I still have. He started talking and I found out he was a lieutenant colonel. He spoke very good English because he was educated at a university near Chicago. He said, 'Why are the Americans fighting the Germans? We should both be joined together to kill the Bolsheviks.'

"I told him that was pure bullshit and we had plenty of reasons to be fighting the Germans. I didn't say it, but I'd heard a lot about what the SS was doing, especially to Jews. When I was a kid growing up, we used to listen to the radio. They had Hitler's speeches. They had reports about *Kristallnacht* and the Gestapo and the storm troopers, stuff about Munich, and other things, so if I didn't know a lot, I wasn't completely ignorant. When things quieted down a little, I jabbed him with the bayonet and pushed him out of the foxhole and back to our lines where he could be interrogated, and I found out they made him take off all his clothes and stand there butt-ass naked, embarrassed, I guess; so he said a lot because, I guess, he figured the war was over for him and what did he have to lose by telling us what he knew. From him, we found out that we were fighting three infantry divisions and one *Volksvan* division and one parachute division."

It would take close to another month, until late November, for the Allies, the American Seventh Army, and the French First Army, with Nyer's unit attached, to make major gains, to fight their way out of the mountains, taking Sam and Tommy close to the German border, to the Rhine River, and to a night that would forever change their lives.

12

Out of the Mountains

The Seventh Army and the French First Army, with Nyer's unit at its side, broke out of the Vosges in November 1944 and raced north. Their goal was to link up with General George Patton's Third Army and drive relentlessly into the German homeland. Intelligence was essential if success were to be achieved, and gathering much of the necessary intelligence fell to the scouts.

"One night the captain called me and Tommy back as we were heading out. He said, 'I want you two to go out tonight and bring back a prisoner, an officer. The generals want a prisoner so they can make sure who we're up against. So, bring back an officer, and bring him back alive.'

"Now, I was looking at the captain and all of a sudden he looked at me and said, 'Nyer, you're a Jew, aren't you?'

"I said, 'Yes,' and in my mind instantaneously I think, here we go again, the damn captain is an anti-Semite. He'd been good to me so I was wondering how that could be. Maybe it was because I was about the only Jew around, and a lot of people had the idea that Jews all landed cushy jobs in the rear, if they even got overseas. But before I could say anything, he says, 'Well, you're going behind enemy lines, and if they capture you they'll kill you because you have an *H* on your dog tags for *Hebrew*. Look, Nyer, let me send your tags back and we'll get them redone.

We'll put on a *P* for *Protestant* so if you're captured you could probably stay alive and live through the war.'

"Before he could say another word, I said, 'Captain, I was born a Jew and I'll die a Jew, and I'm not changing my tags and I'm not giving up the mezuzah around my neck, and I'm not taking it off.'

"So Tommy and me go out and we got behind German lines and we were crawling and freezing. Now, it's November, and in Europe, like in America, they pile up the corn like an Indian teepee to dry it out. We were between the American German lines and Tommy said, 'I got to have a smoke.'

"I said, 'If you light up, we're going to get shot, because they'll see the light and they'll come down on us.'

"He said, 'I got to have a smoke.'

"I said, 'Tommy, you're not smoking here. Hold off.'

'He said, 'I can't. I have to have a smoke.'

"So, finally I gave in, and we went inside that corn teepee thing and he sat down on my knees, his body braced against my chest, and he's smoking away, and all of a sudden we heard a German patrol coming along. It sounded like five or eight men, and they stopped maybe thirty feet away. I could hardly breathe, but I don't say a word because noise carries in the dark. I'm holding my breath, and the next thing I know I'm outside lying in the snow and he's pulling me up. I was unconscious from holding my breath too long. I said, 'What happened to the Germans?'

"He said, 'They left. You've been out here for two minutes. I pulled you out of the teepee. I thought you was dead.'

"So then we start out again to get that prisoner. I figure we got about one hundred feet behind their lines, in the rear echelon, where we saw some cooks and other nonfighting German soldiers. All of a sudden against a tree we see this officer smoking a cigarette, and he had a field cap on instead of a helmet.

We're hiding behind this bush. I whisper to Tommy, 'What the hell are we going to do? This is the kind of officer they want us to capture, so how are we going to do it?' I mean, we didn't have rifles or pistols, because that would have brought the whole Germany Army down on us, and we'd have been horse meat in ten seconds. What we had were knives, brass knuckles, and a little bar that you could knock a guy out. I had a pistol, but I sure wasn't going to use it unless there was an emergency. So I said, 'I'll sneak up behind the tree, and you sneak a little to my right and rustle, and he'll turn, he'll move away from the tree to see what's going on, and then I'll whack him on the head and we'll pull him out.' Which is just what happened. First I thought I'd hit him so hard he was dead, but then he started moaning, so we grabbed him and pulled him through the shrubbery and through the German lines. He was still moaning, so I gave him another whack, and he started to bleed a little and went completely unconscious. Now we're dragging him through the snow and he's dead weight, and we've got a couple of hundred yards to go, and it's freezing.

"Tommy says, 'Let's leave him here. We're killing ourselves, and it'll be daylight in another half-hour.'

"I said, 'No, Tommy, if we don't get him back very soon, we'll leave him, but we've got to try.' Fortunately, we were right close to the American lines, so we start yelling who we are because we forgot the password. The guys came up and so we brought back the officer they wanted. And they gave us medals for that. Later they offered me a battlefield commission. I turned it down. I never wanted to be an officer in the first place. And I was still a scout. First scout is what they called me."

13

Plunder

The French First Army, with Nyer's unit still at its side, advanced deeper into Alsace. To the north, the German Army was massing for a counteroffensive in the Ardennes, the Battle of the Bulge, that would begin in mid-December and would rage for weeks, the outcome in doubt, until the weather cleared and the Allies could once more take the offensive.

But the French had other things on their minds. On November 23, 1944, the troops reached the historic city of Strasbourg, a prize the French desperately wanted to reclaim and which the Germans were just as determined to hold, considering it German, considering it part of Greater Germany. The honor of leading the attack and liberating the city was given to General Philippe LeClerc, one of General Charles de Gaulle's closest and more trusted officers. He had previously been given the honor of leading the French in the liberation of Paris.

"I had spent the last two months fighting my way across France and all I ever saw were bombed-out towns and deserted villages," Nyer says. "That day, looking down on that town, it was a different sight. It didn't look damaged at all. It just looked pretty."

The plan was to take Strasbourg without the softening up of an artillery barrage. "Somebody over at HQ decided that getting that place back should be a totally French job. That was fine with us, because as far as we were concerned they hadn't done much fighting until then, and we figured since this was their country, they ought to do some of the work. Then we learned that one of the French generals who was going to lead the attack had been born in the area and he didn't like idea of our bombs falling on his town. That was just crazy. Trying to take a fortified place is one hell of a job in the best of times, but to go into battle with no artillery cover was suicide. But if that was what the French wanted, good luck to them.

"Then my company commander, who's been talking to a French general, calls me over and tells me that Tommy and I are going to be lead scouts for them, and we'd have no artillery and no tank cover. That was about the last thing I wanted to hear. He wanted us to go out with no cover and show them the way. So I said to the French general, 'Why do you need American scouts leading your troops if this is supposed to be a completely French effort?'

"The French general heard that and he didn't like that, and he sure as hell didn't like me for asking that question. So he turned to my captain and he said, very serious-like, 'Are all your troops this undisciplined?'

"The captain starts screaming at me and he orders me to go over and wait by his Jeep. As I'm moving away, he says to the French general, 'The kid's right. Why don't you have your own scouts?'

"Let me tell you, this captain was a good man. He used to say Tommy and I were his walking miracles. Here we are, two outcasts in the Army, me, a tall, skinny, Jewish kid from New York, and Tommy, a short, feisty Indian from some godforsaken tribe, and we're still alive and kicking. So the captain wasn't anxious for us to be taking any more risks than we had to. He was a good man, and what happened to him in the war got to him and later he took to drink, which killed him."

That night, Sam Nyer and Tommy DeLion moved out toward Strasbourg. They were about five hundred yards ahead of the French troops. "They figured we were the experts and once we found the best way into town, we'd get word back to them, and they'd follow."

Nyer and Tommy DeLion found an opening in the walls, and signaled back to the French that the way was clear. The French began the assault.

For a day and a night and on into the next day, the battle for control of the ancient city raged. Supplies were brought up from the rear and the battle resumed until finally Strasbourg was back in the hands of the French. There were rumors that, with the victory, some of the American troops went on a looting spree while the French were more concerned with consolidating their hold on this prize. But then, looting, especially of the plunder that the Germans had amassed, had become more the rule than the exception, and while American commanders frowned on it and threatened reprisals if they caught the looters, their warnings tended to be ignored.

Strasbourg might be French once more, but the Allies' hold on the city was tenuous. German strongholds had been established to the north and south, and Allied intelligence was reporting large concentrations of German forces massing in the woods across the Rhine. There was a possibility, even a probability, that a counteroffensive was about to be launched. And so began the Battle of the Bulge in the Ardennes to the north. By late December, the German offensive in the Ardennes was collapsing with the return of clear weather—giving the Allies control of the skies—and the arrival of reinforcements, especially General George Patton's Third Army. With the Allied armies heavily engaged in the Ardennes, now attention began to focus on Alsace. The defenses against another possible German assault north and south of Strasbourg were stretched thin: General Patch's Seventh Army with six divisions and the French First Army were arrayed in a line stretching 126 miles along the Rhine and north to the Saarbrücken area. If the Germans attacked in force, they might well be able to punch a hole in those Allied defenses, split the Seventh Army, trap elements in the tightening ring, and recapture Strasbourg.

That, indeed, was the German plan. Called Operation Nordwind, it would be the last German offensive of the war. On New Year's Day 1945, the German Nineteenth Army drove northeast out of a bridgehead in Colmar, while the German First Army attacked across the Rhine through a bridgehead at Gambsheim toward Bitche in the north of Alsace. Despite intelligence reports of the buildup, the assault took the Allies by surprise. As they had in the Ardennes, the Germans made serious inroads into Allied positions. At that point, General Dwight D. Eisenhower considered ceding Strasbourg to the Germans and falling back to the foothills of the Vosges. The French were appalled. They rejected with such vehemence the idea of relinquishing Strasbourg that Eisenhower abandoned his plan and threw forces into both the defenses around Bitche and into what was called the Colmar Pocket.

To meet the initial attack, some units of the French Army turned south toward the cities and towns along the Rhine, while others turned north. Nyer's company and elements of the French First Army moved into position on a hill overlooking an ancient village near the Rhine. Nyer was never sure of its name, nor its exact location on a map, as he was rarely sure just where he was. If his unit had moved south, it was most likely either Erstein or Gershteim. More likely, it had gone north, toward Gambsheim, about fifteen miles from Strasbourg, an ancient fortified town at the juncture of the Rhine and the Zorn Rivers, ringed with streams and canals, approached across bridges, and hard by a heavily forested area. (There are times when Nyer thinks the town was farther west—Jebsheim, which became the center of action at the end of January—but, given his own time frame, Gambsheim seems most likely.) All were considered German by the Germans, though they had not yet been incorporated into the Reich; they were still within the conquered and occupied territories, and all had escaped major destruction since the German blitzkrieg of 1940. Gambsheim, however, was at the center of the new German counteroffensive and was the scene of major fighting.

Once more, Nyer and Tommy DeLion led the way into the town. In the darkness before midnight, they reached the walls. "We were told we were to take this little bridge across what I think was a moat, or maybe a canal, and then find a way over the walls. The thing was, there were two German machine gunners on either side of the bridge and we couldn't have any artillery fire to help us. So we moved up, very quiet, and we took them out without much trouble, then gave the signal back to the French and our troops what we'd done so they could move up."

Once the bridge was cleared, they crept against the town wall, found a hole in it, and wriggled their way through and into the town. Fighting between French and American and German forces erupted behind them, but for a time they were ahead of the battle.

After about two hours, the fighting began to die down. The Germans still held half the town and the Allies, the other half, but ammunition was running low. After a few hours, the fighting subsided as both the Germans and the Allies fell back to regroup and wait for new supplies. In the suddenly eerily quiet town, Sam Nyer and Tommy DeLion moved silently down a main street, hugging the building walls, Sam on the left side of the street, Tommy on the right, the way they always did whenever they moved through an enemy city—not speaking, using nods, whistles, and hand signals, a code they had developed over time. Sam covered Tommy, his eyes studying the rooftops and corners, Tommy watching the windows and doorways.

"We got about halfway down this street when Tommy gives me the signal that he sees something in this building right ahead of me. Three fingers raised, like the sees three Germans. I see what looks like some sort of official building with large windows and a heavy oak door. The door's open a little and at first glance the place looks deserted, but there's a little light around the edges of the windows. I lean forward to kick in the door and in one quick move throw the two grenades I had strung from my glasses into the room. A couple of seconds later we hear the booms and then we heard some groaning and screaming. We expect whoever's inside to start shooting back at us. But nothing happens. We just keep hearing those groans from inside.

"We charge into the room and I get my back up against the wall closest to me while Tommy keeps running past me. God, he was fast. He makes it to the other side of the room in a heartbeat. Then we wait and let our eyes adjust to the dark. We keep waiting, and nothing happens.

"But our eyes get used to the dark and on the far side of the room I can make out a huge safe with the door standing open. I think maybe we're in some kind of bank.

"Meanwhile, we keep hearing these groans. I see who's making all the noise. There they were, three soldiers, officers from the look of them, lying next to each other on the floor next to those safety deposit boxes. Tommy notices them, too, and we decide not to take any chances. We fire more rounds into them. Of course, it wasn't necessary. They were already dead, or if they weren't dead yet, they were once we fired into them.

"Now we move closer to them, and I realize they're not the Wehrmacht troops we were used to seeing in battle. These guys are much older than the kids they put on the front lines, and they're dressed in dark black uniforms with a skull and cross-bones sewn on their chest pockets. The uniforms were immaculate. There wasn't a speck of dirt on them anywhere, just the blood now from where our bullets and the grenades ripped into them.

"Then Tommy points out that they got no weapons, just pistols, Lugers, in holsters, which was pretty strange. I look at their uniforms and their polished shoes, trying to figure out who they were. Then I realize. They're fuckin' SS. Then I see that the one closest to the entrance has this big brown carpetbag lying right beside him

"I tell Tommy I think we're in a bank. And I tell him maybe we can find some French money in here, which makes his eyes light up. Not for the value of the money but because those big soft French notes were the only thing we had for toilet paper. In war, you get used to certain things, like not having a shower or not sleeping in a soft bed. But you never get used to doing your business without decent toilet paper. And the French money was the best damn toilet paper I ever used. In fact, all we ever wanted when we entered a house after a battle was to find a big stack of this fine French money.

"Now, there we were, Tommy and me and these three dead Germans and a heavy brown suitcase sitting in this blown-up room. And outside we can hear the French troops and some of our own moving into the street, and we can hear shots and explosions, so we figured the fighting was beginning again.

"We keep looking at that satchel. I try to pick it up. There was a chain locked around the handle. So Tommy pried the chain off the handles and I picked it up, not expecting it to be as heavy as it was. It must have weighed at least twenty pounds. For some reason, I don't know why, because I'd never taken anything before, I grabbed the satchel and we ran out of the place."

Sam Nyer and Tommy DeLion had walked in on a looting scene, the SS looting the loot that had been gathered from the exterminated of Eastern Europe and from the diamond centers of Antwerp and Amsterdam, plunder the SS had stored for its own use in private depositories in Strasbourg and in some of the nearby towns both north and south of that city. They obviously thought these towns would be even safer than Strasbourg, places where nobody, certainly not their superiors back in Berlin, would ever have thought to investigate. With their Nazi empire collapsing around them, with Strasbourg already fallen to the Allies, and with it the private repositories of all the treasures that had been piled there, these three SS officers had most likely decided it was time to take off with what they could, with the best, and so had journeyed the short distance to this town where a secret cache had been established. And so they had opened the safe, knowing just what was in it, removed what they wanted, and heaped their treasures in the valise, and most probably had a boat waiting to carry them down the Rhine to safety in Switzerland. The two Americans had interrupted them at the last moment.

As Nyer and DeLion reached the street, the fighting erupted again. The battle was brutal and there were heavy casualties on both sides. And then it died down once more, the Germans retreating as the Americans brought up tanks and heavy artillery.

"We came to a separation in the center of the city," Nyer remembers. "There was a cement wall. We sat down next to it along with the other guys in our squad. I put the satchel down next to me and I said to Tommy, 'I'm going to open it.' Some of the other guys gathered around. On top were stacks of French francs, the best toilet paper in the world, and underneath were stacks of German marks. And underneath were diamond rings and bracelets and all kinds of gold and silver jewelry. Everybody wanted some and they started grabbing the money and the jewelry and everything else. And they moved away with what they had taken. Then we noticed the satchel had a false bottom. Tommy kicked it in, and in that bottom was a big purple chamois bag, as big as a melon. There were gold letters burned into the top of it. I opened it and inside were these big what looked like rocks. I figured they had something more than rocks, so I looked at them and I realized they were diamonds, uncut diamonds. There were forty of them and some were as big as hazelnuts, some as big as a walnut, some even bigger, and some were white and some had colors in them. I couldn't believe my eyes."

In later years, remembering this moment and relating it to others, spinning this story that night in Bangor to Yaron Svoray, there would be times when Sam Nyer would be sure that the gold letters on that pouch spelled the word *Kimberly*, the diamond mines in South Africa. At other times, though, as the years passed, he thought perhaps the letters on the pouch were not *Kimberly* but *KZ V . . .* , though he couldn't remember what came after the *V*.

"I said, 'Tommy, these are worth a lot of money. What do you want to do with them? Tommy, we're rich!' He wasn't impressed. I wasn't sure if he understood what it meant to be rich. To him things like that had no meaning. In his mind, France and wherever he was from were the same place, just with different white people living there. Now, I knew I couldn't carry all these diamonds by myself, so I needed to convince him it was worthwhile to take them. I asked him if he wanted some, but he said he wasn't interested. He said he wouldn't know what to do with them, which was probably true. So I tried to explain to him that the diamonds would make him a happy man. He didn't care. Finally, I got mad. I said I wouldn't be his friend if he didn't take half. You know what he did? He just shrugged. Because he knew that any extra weight we carried might get us killed. He was right, of course. Moving ahead of the troops scouting, we had to be able to react fast and anything that got in our way could be the difference between life and death. But I understood the value of those diamonds outside the war, and I made sure I got my point across to him. I said, 'Tommy, with just one of those stones you can buy yourself a whole truckload of cigarettes.' Now, that got to him, being a chain-smoker. And that's how I got him to carry half the diamonds.

"I took twenty stones and put them into the leather pouch and then I tied the strings of the pouch to my belt and tucked the pouch inside my pants. Tommy took out a filthy red bandana from his pocket, tied it around the other twenty diamonds, and shoved the bundle back into his pocket.

The diamonds now shared by Sam Nyer and Tommy DeLion, the francs, marks, and the rest of the treasure split among the other members of the platoon, somebody hung the now empty stachel from a tree and everybody took turns firing at it until it was shredded.

"I guess you could call what we did looting, though I think of it as liberating what the Germans had looted. But what the hell, it was war and where did the stuff come from in the first place? Wasn't it all loot the Nazis had grabbed from everywhere in Europe, from people they were killing? So maybe it was like tit for tat. How can you loot from a looter? Anyway, a couple of days after we split all the stuff, the captain gathers the company out in a square and he says there's word that the troops have been looting and the army won't stand for that. So what he wants us to do is pile up everything we'd taken and heap it in the middle of the square. He says he'll turn his back so he won't know who was doing the looting, but he wants us to give the stuff back. Now, he turns his back for a couple of minutes. Nobody moves. And when he turns around, there's nothing in the square, no pile, no loot, not a damn thing. And that was that."

At this point in telling his story to Svoray, Sam Nyer paused, a look of anguish and frustration on his face. "From the minute we got those diamonds, our lives changed. I wish we'd never found them. Damn diamonds. They were cursed."

14

Killing Fields

The battle at Gambsheim proved indecisive, a stalemate at first, and then the Germans gradually moved forward. The French First Army was more concerned with defending Strasbourg than anything else, and it headed back that way. Nyer's unit and other elements of the Seventh Army were sped to Bitche, and began not merely a defense but a counterattack against the Germans, an attack that halted the German advances and sent the Wehrmacht reeling back.

"While we were walking through this town, Bitche, someone on a doorstep yelled out, 'Hey, Sam, what are you doing here?' I walked over to this man, and he was someone I'd trained with in the field artillery, and he was still in the field artillery. He looked at me and he said, 'What the hell are you doing in the infantry?'

"I said, 'What are you still doing in the artillery?'

"He said, 'I've always been in the artillery, since Fort Bragg.'

"I said, 'You're one lucky man. Bless yourself.'"

Once the Germans were repelled at Bitche, Nyer's unit headed southwest for the Colmar Pocket. The Allied aim was to link up with other Allied forces engaged in the struggle, capture the small village of Jebsheim in the center of the pocket, and quash this German assault.

"One day, when we were holding against a German counter-attack which had pushed back our lines a couple of hundred feet, the captain called me back and said, 'Sam, I want you to take twelve men and knock out those two German machine guns that are holding us up.'

"I said, 'Captain, that's murder in this snow. Only twelve men, and we're at the point where we can't get much protection from our artillery or our own machine guns. Let me do it to-night. Hold the attack and I'll take a couple of men and we'll knock out those machine guns, and then the whole company can move up.'

"He said, 'It has to be done now.'

"I said, 'Whose orders?'

"He said, 'It comes from regimental headquarters, from the colonel.'

"I said, 'So you lead the attack, captain.'

'He said, 'No, I'm ordering you. That's an order.'

"You get an order in war, you obey the order; otherwise you get a court-martial. What choice did I have? I said, 'Captain, this is murder. Men you're giving me are replacements, they don't have much experience and they don't know what to do. They've never experienced combat, and you want me to take these twelve men and do this thing. At least, can you give me some help?'

"He said, 'I'll give you some machine-gun fire on each flank until you get to about two hundred feet, and then I can't do it anymore, because we'll be killing our own men.'

"I knew I'd have to do what I was ordered. Maybe we'd get lucky, though I had my doubts. We unloaded our backpacks and any unnecessary equipment, and I took the twelve men and I explained what we had to do. I said, 'You're going to have to learn fast because your lives depend on it. Just remember this.

German machine gunners can't fire for more than twenty or thirty seconds; otherwise they'll burn out their barrels. So they give quick bursts. The minute it stops, you've got about ten seconds to get up and run toward the machine guns before they start firing again. Only, don't run straight. Run at an angle so they can't take a direct bead on you. Stay at least twenty or thirty feet apart. When you drop to the snow, roll at least ten feet, because the machine gunners will be aiming where you dropped. If you want to stay alive, stay apart, run as fast as you can in the time you have but at an angle, and never forget how long you have for each run."

Under Nyer's command, his dozen replacements moved out, advancing about four hundred feet from the German lines. "I'm worried about my own life. I'm not worried about anybody else's. I'm running toward the German machine guns and I'm ducking and waving, and while I'm doing that, I'm looking left and right, and there's only a couple of guys, and we're down to six men out of twelve. We get up and we run, and as I'm dropping to the snow, I'm looking left and there's nobody there, and on the right there's one man left. And here I am, two hundred feet from two German machine guns. I can't run back because they'll kill me, and I'm exhausted from running, and it's cold and I'm freezing and my fingers are numb, and every time I hit the ground the diamonds in the pouch inside my belt jabbed into me and bruised my side, which began to hurt like hell. Maybe I should have ditched them. They seemed to weigh a ton, and I guess they were slowing me down. But I never thought about doing that. There was no way I was going to give them up. I checked my ammunition and I only had twenty rounds left, so I told myself I'm going to hold my fire until I get close enough, and then it'll be semiautomatic, not automatic. I'm within seventy feet of those machine guns and the guy on my right gets hit, and then something hits my helmet and knocks me to the ground. All it does is knock my helmet off and give me a good bruise, and maybe I was bleeding a little, but I'm hidden by the snow.

"I could hear one of the Germans ask the other, *'Es is tot?'*— Is he dead? And the other says, *'Ja.'* I hear the machine gun turning away from me. I'm lying in the snow and my head is killing me, and my helmet's knocked off and there's blood on my head. I said to myself, 'You're either going to stay here and freeze because you can't make it back, or you're going to have to kill six men with one bullet.' I was preparing to die, but I was going to take as many as I could with me. I'm lying in the snow and I finally gather some strength. I unbuckle my knife and loosen my ammo belt to get as much weight off as possible. I figure I can run at least fifty feet before they know I'm on them. I steeled myself and I got up and started to run toward the machine gun, and about twenty-five feet away they reacted and started to swing the machine gun around toward me. I shot the first three guys at the first machine gun. They just fell over. I pulled the trigger. I thought it was on semiautomatic, but it was on automatic, and the rounds went out as I'm running, and I'm ten feet away from the other three guys, and I pull the trigger and there's a click. I'm out of ammo. I'm thinking well, I'll kill one or two with the barrel, and the third one's going to be a problem. But just as I'm thinking that, they raised their hands, and I took them prisoner and got them back to our lines, and then we were able to mount an attack.

"I got recommended for a Silver Star for that. Only, like I told the captain, it was murder in the snow for the twelve new guys he sent out with me: four had got killed and the rest wounded."

The German offensive in the Colmar Pocket, and the entire Operation Nordwind, was broken by the end of January 1945. The Americans then proceeded to fight their way north after the retreating Wehrmacht.

One night during the march, as Nyer and DeLion huddled for shelter in a foxhole, someone came to Nyer with an idea.

"We'd been fighting in France for a couple of months when I ran into Sergeant Wolfe. This was while we were fighting in the mountains. He was older, maybe around thirty. I met him first back in the States during basic, and here he was again."

From Wolfe, Sam Nyer heard the latest rumors about what the Nazis were doing to the Jews and the kind of anti-Semitism a Jew faced on the front lines. Then, as the Army moved toward Colmar, they lost contact, though Nyer began to hear stories that at Strasbourg, Wolfe and his squad of twelve men had broken into a bank and looted it. Nobody gave that much thought, since others had done the same thing, but some guys said that in the time that followed, Wolfe and his unit changed, grew more wary, more cautious, tried to stay as far from the action as possible, and somehow stayed intact, suffering no losses. That was remarkable. They were in battle, because it was impossible to avoid battle, and yet nobody in that unit got killed. Nobody even got wounded.

Then, on this January night, Wolfe suddenly reappeared. He seemed, Nyer remembers, very tired and much older.

"I want to speak to you," Wolfe said. "Alone."

"Don't worry about Tommy," Nyer told him. "He doesn't speak good English, and even if he understood, he wouldn't give a damn."

While Tommy sat and smoked on one side the foxhole, Wolfe began to tell Nyer that the major assault on Germany would begin as soon as they reached the German border and enough fresh recruits arrived.

Everybody knew that, Nyer said.

The battles would be fierce, Wolfe said, and there would be

major casualties because once the border was crossed, the Germans would be fighting for their homeland, not for occupied territory, and they would fight to the last man. "I don't want any part of it," Wolfe said. "I don't want to get killed and I don't want my boys to get killed. We've gotten this far without losing a man, and I want it to stay that way."

"What are you going to do about it?" Nyer asked.

"We're leaving. Very soon. I'm inviting you to come along. Because I like you and besides, you're a scout, and you can help us find the best way out."

Wolfe was talking desertion, which could mean court-martial at the very least, and possibly a firing squad. Nyer wanted no part of it. He told Wolfe to forget the whole idea and get some rest, and everything would work out. Wolfe shook his head, grasped Nyer's hand, said they'd meet when the war was over, and walked away. That was the last time Nyer would see Wolfe. The next morning, the sergeant and his men were gone.

A couple of days later, two officers, clean and freshly shaven, uniforms unblemished, appeared. They said they were investigating the disappearance of Sergeant Wolfe and his twelve-man squad. Did anyone, they asked, have any idea what had become of them? Had they been sent out on a mission and failed to return? Did anyone know? No one claimed to have any knowledge.

Then someone mentioned Nyer and that he knew Wolfe. The two officers approached Nyer and put their questions to him. "They had a condescending attitude and they started making anti-Semitic remarks," Nyer remembers, "so I kept my mouth shut and didn't give them the time of day. Besides, they were from back at headquarters, nice and safe, so nobody had any use for them, and nobody said a word."

The officers went their way, unenlightened. For the next few days, the disappearance of Wolfe and his men was the center of every conversation. There were some who said they were sure Wolfe and his squad had been sent into Germany on a secret mission. Others claimed they had escaped to Switzerland or maybe Paris with the loot they taken from a bank in Strasbourg, which might have been true, since looting had been widespread. And then, as preparation for the assault into Germany accelerated, attention turned elsewhere.

By early February, Nyer's company reached the small city of Sarreguemines in Alsace, overlooking the Saar River on the border between France and Germany. At that point, the company was detached from the French and rejoined the U.S. Seventh Army as Company F, 254th Regiment, 63rd Infantry, Second Battalion.

"Every night after we found the diamonds, me and Tommy would find us a safe spot and count our diamonds and dream about our lives after the war. We sort of organized ourselves into a routine. During the day, in the middle of the fighting, all we'd think about was making it to the next sunset, and at night we'd play with the diamonds, trying to believe there was something worth living for. I'd think about cars and girls and a big house with lots of rooms. I don't know what Tommy dreamed about, probably just tons and tons of cigarettes."

They arrived in Sarreguemines just after midnight. "It was very eerie and it was very dark. We crossed a bridge, made a left, and people started to come out onto the front steps of their houses and watch us as we went by. Some of them had American flags and some had Nazi flags. They weren't waving. They were just watching us as we marched by. We went through the town, past some manufacturing plants on the outskirts, past some heaps of sulfur, and we went by a church at the fork in the road. I remember that in front of the church there was a statue of the Virgin Mary kneeling beside the cross on which her son was being crucified. We marched about three miles past the town and then we came to a field. We were told to go across one at a time because there was a minefield that hadn't been cleaned out. Actually, we went through six minefields, one at a time, and finally we reached this hill, and they put us in some empty foxholes, which we were told were occupied by the French in World War I.

"Then, there we were, in our little foxhole on a knoll in this forest less than a mile from the Saar, Germany just across the river. All around us, in maybe thirty or forty other foxholes, there were other guys. We all dug in, reinforced our foxholes—ringed them with barbed wire, did everything we could to make them safe for us—because we knew we were going to be there for a while before we made our move into Germany, and if the Germans counterattacked us, we wanted as much protection as we could get."

For about three weeks, they remained on that hill, in those woods, waiting while fresh troops arrived daily and were deployed in all the hills and forests in the area, digging into those old French foxholes, preparing for the massive thrust that would lead to the final battles of the war, lead to victory and a return home. During the next twenty days, Sam Nyer and Tommy DeLion counted their diamonds, played with them, and studied, memorized, the area around them. From their foxhole high on their hill, near the crest, they could see through the trees, now barren of leaves in winter, a river meandering at the base of the hill. Sam Nyer thought the river was the Saar. It was, in fact, the Blies River, and there was a small town on the banks of the river occupied by the Germans, a town whose name Nyer never knew. From their foxhole, they could make out on their right a church steeple, too large, Nyer thought, for such a small town; and then, moving from his vantage point toward his left, a ruined farmhouse and other farm structures, a field, a small bridge crossing the river, other landmarks. Studying the terrain was a way of passing time. And they kept hearing of the arrival of more and more troops. It was about time, Sam Nyer thought.

There were guys around him who dreamed of going home, talked about it constantly. Nyer was one of them. But he was sure he would get home only when the war was over, or if he were wounded, or in a coffin. He had no intention of shooting himself in the foot or inflicting on himself some other small, disabling wound that would mean the end of the war for him. He was in it for the duration, as long as he managed to stay alive. With the major offensive into Germany about to begin, the odds against that grew ever larger.

15

A Hole in a Foxhole

In the forest overlooking the French-German border in Alsace, the days and nights for Sam Nyer and Tommy DeLion were filled not merely with waiting in their foxhole, counting their diamonds, dreaming of what they would do with them when the war was over, and memorizing the environment. There were skirmishes, there were attacks and counterattacks, there was constant peril.

"When we landed in France, we had thousands of men in our unit," Nyer recalls. "By the time they shipped the unit back home, there were less than two thirds able-bodied soldiers left from my original outfit. The rest were either dead or wounded, or missing in action.

"I didn't want to be one of them. And I was getting afraid that was where I was heading. I was doing what they asked, but I knew I was turning into a bad soldier. I mean, all I could think about were those diamonds and what I was going to do with them. I couldn't concentrate on anything else. I was preoccupied. Those diamonds were becoming a real pain in the ass. Much as I liked counting them and touching them, they were making me uncomfortable. Every time I fell to the ground, they'd give me a bruise right where they were, in that pouch against my side. So I kept thinking about that, kept trying to fall so I wouldn't hurt myself, worrying about things I shouldn't have been worrying about. I knew that a soldier who can't concentrate on his job is very soon a dead soldier. I knew we had to do something. It was time to get back to being a scout, to finish this war properly."

Early in the evening of February 23, 1945, Nyer's commanding officer summoned him. Across the Blies, which Nyer still believed to be the Saar, the Germans were dug in, hidden in shelters in the village and in the forests rising beyond it. With the attack impending, the captain told Nyer it was essential to learn what the Army would be facing. Nyer and DeLion, he ordered, were to circle the town, Blies Schmeyen, though nobody then knew its name, and try to discover what forces the Germans had massed, what defensive positions they had taken.

"Tommy and I scrambled down over a steep side and into a valley and crossed the river. It was night, naturally, and pitch black. We finally got behind the town, and we heard noises, and we knew there must be tanks in the town. We were there only about a half an hour, but what we figured out was there must have been two or three German companies in the area, six hundred or seven hundred men, and we were sure there were at least a couple of tanks there, too.

"Then we scrambled back across the river and up the hill and reported what we'd learned to the captain.

"That night, when we got back to our foxhole, I decided it was time to hide the diamonds. I felt that this was as good a place to hide them as any other. So I tell Tommy, this is it, this is where we bury the diamonds, here, inside our foxhole. I knew we could always find our way back to this foxhole to dig them up. When you stay in one place for two or three weeks and all you do all day every day is study the landscape, from every tree to every farmhouse, know the curve of the river and how the mountains look at every minute of the day, you remember; you never forget.

"We dug through most of the night. We dug on the left side of the foxhole. I don't know why we chose that side, it just happened. The ground was hard and heavy and frozen, seeing it was still winter, and it was hard to dig, especially with a small shovel and a knife. But we kept digging and by the time the sun came up, we were down about three feet. I tell Tommy to hand over his diamonds, which he did. I put them with mine in that purple leather pouch, just as we had found them, and dropped them into the hole, and I added the couple of gold things I'd kept and a couple of letters my father wrote to me, which was a perfect way of saying this was mine, this was my hole, and what was in it belonged to me. Then we filled the hole back in with dirt and put a piece of barbed wire across it before anyone else got up.

"Do you know what was strange right then? From the moment we buried the diamonds, we never spoke about them again. Not once. Of course, we didn't have much of a chance to ever talk about them again. You know why? Because the very next morning we got ourselves a new officer. Our old first lieutenant was badly wounded the previous week. So they send us this idiot right out of OCS, a ninety-day wonder, fresh off the boat and looking for medals. He says he wants to get some Germans before the war's over. God, we knew his kind. There were a lot of them on the front lines and they never lasted very long. They kept making mistakes and getting a lot of our guys killed for nothing.

"He called me and Tommy over to him from our foxhole up

to the crest of the hill and introduced himself, and we took one look at him and we knew right then that he was strictly bad news. His uniform was new and starched and his helmet doesn't have a scratch on it. Everything about him was shiny. Including his rifle. We're crouching low, keeping down so we don't get our heads blown off in case there are snipers over there, and this new commanding officer is strutting around like he's on parade. I'm thinking, this guy's crazy. But I don't worry much because I figure he'll be dead in a day or two.

"He takes me and leads me down the hill to the edge of the forest, to the forward observer positions, while Tommy goes back to our foxhole. He asks me to tell him exactly what we'd seen when Tommy and me went behind the town the previous night, and what we guessed. I told him. He takes out his field glasses and he studies the town, and he says, 'There's a German tiger tank with its nose sticking out behind the church.' Then he says, 'I'm going to call up the artillery and we're going to knock down that tank.'

"I ask him if we're going into battle. He says, no, but the battle will start in a few days and he just wants to scare the Germans. I can't believe what I'm hearing. This moron wants to shell the Germans to scare them? I mean, he thinks the Germans who've been fighting for six years are going to suddenly get scared by a couple of artillery rounds? So, I say to him, 'If you start shelling them, they'll start shelling us, and we're going to lose men. You can't do it, lieutenant. If we're not going to launch a full attack, why bother at all? If you want to take out those tanks, we'll figure a way. Tommy and I can do it if we have to.'

"He looks at me with his dull brown eyes, which made me think he was literally an idiot. So I add, 'We should only bomb when we're ready to move. Otherwise, it will just start an artillery duel, and we could lose a lot of men.'

"He gets up and turns around, picks up his walkie-talkie, and yells into it that he wants a barrage to start on the German positions. It was eleven o'clock in the morning. I knew right then that he'd be responsible for many casualties. Just as I predicted, as soon as we launched our artillery attack, the Germans began their own. Just like that, the forest became a killing zone. It was such a waste of lives.

"I grabbed my rifle, jumped up from that forward position, and raced back toward our foxhole. I was just about there when I felt something hit me in my back. It was like being hit by a sledgehammer. A shell exploded on a tree right beside the foxhole and knocked me into it, and I landed right on top of Tommy and the tree trunk landed on top of me, and I had this terrible pain in my side. I was nearly unconscious.

"The next thing I knew, Tommy was standing next to me. Mortar rounds and bombs were falling all around us. I said, 'Tommy, I think I got hit.'

"He said, 'Where?'

"I said, 'Take a look at the front. See if you see any blood or anything.' I was getting a little numb.

"He felt around and he said, 'No. There's nothing there.'

"I said, 'I wonder what happened? I can hardly breathe and I'm in agony, in pain. Look somewhere else. Maybe I'm wounded somewhere else.'

"He started to look at my back. He said, 'Oh, you got a little hole in your field jacket.'

"I said, 'A little hole? Rip it open and see what's there.'

"He started to rip, and the hole got bigger and bigger. Finally he said, 'You're bleeding.' And he started to yell for the medic. He yelled loud enough. Even with all the sounds around you, it carried. My tiny partner pulled me out from under the tree trunk and out of the foxhole. A medic came up, and my head was swimming, and I was, like, coming in and out of consciousness. But I could sort of hear what was being said. Tommy said to him, 'Look at his back.'

"The medic looked at it and he said, 'He's got a bad wound. We'll have to get him out quick.' So they called for more help to bring a stretcher in. As they were putting me on the stretcher, I looked at Tommy for the last time. It was the last time I ever saw him. I grabbed his hand and we sort of shook hands. Tommy asked the medic something, and he said, 'He's got a mortal wound.' And then they carried me off. I looked back once and Tommy was standing there, staring at me.

"I was conscious the whole time, but I couldn't speak or move. The pain was so bad I wanted to die then and there, and if I could've spoken, I would've asked them to shoot me and put me out of my misery."

Sam Nyer had been hit by shrapnel that ripped through his back and lodged less than an inch from his spinal cord. By the time he reached the evacuation center, he was nearly dead. The medics took one look at his blood-soaked body and made the assessment that he could not survive. There were casualties pouring in who seemed to have a better chance, so they would be the first to receive treatment. It was called triage—the wounded were classified by possibility of survival: Those most likely to live were treated first, those with some chance were treated second, and those with no chance were ignored until everybody else was taken care of, which, for all practical purposes, was never. Nyer was in the third category. He was laid on a stretcher outside the hospital tent, left alone to die.

"I stayed on that stretcher for a long time. They kept checking, sure I was going to die any second. But I didn't, and finally one of the nurses noticed that I was still breathing. She gave me plasma and sulfur and shots of morphine and then they took me to the hospital in Metz. They strapped me in the front of an ambulance and I was hurting so bad I was bending over. I couldn't sit up straight, and I said, 'Have you got anything for the pain?' They gave me some more morphine. In the meantime, I heard the guys in the back of the ambulance talking. They were twin brothers, and they'd stepped on a mine, and one lost his left leg and the other lost his right leg; and even in the pain they were in and as doped up as they were, they were talking, and one of them said to the other, 'We only need one pair of shoes now.'

"I thought that was funny. They're lying down, talking like that, and I'm sitting up, and I'm figuring I'm bleeding to death, and I can't stand the pain. Then the ambulance hit a big bump or a shell hole or something, and my head hit the windshield and knocked me out. When I woke up, I was lying on a stretcher in Metz, and there were hundreds of men on stretchers groaning, the bleeding all around. It looked like the Civil War in Atlanta in *Gone with the Wind*. A nurse came over and said, 'Are you in pain?' I said, 'I can't stand the pain any longer.' She gave me another shot of morphine, and ten minutes later she gave me another shot, and then she brought a doctor over. He looked at me and he said, 'Where he's wounded? The morphine isn't helping. Take him upstairs to the operating room.' There were six or seven operations going on at the same time. The surgeon came over to me and I said, 'Am I going to live?' He said, 'Yes, you're going to be okay.' They gave me something to knock me out and the next thing I knew I was in a bed with white sheets, which I hadn't seen in eight months. The guy in the next bed said, 'They pulled the sheets over your head twice already. They thought you were dead.'

"They patched me up some, and then shipped me to another hospital in Dijon and then to one in England where I spent a year recuperating. Then, when they thought I could survive the trip, they shipped me back to the States. I spent another year and a half in different hospitals and finally made it back home with my discharge and a couple of Purple Hearts and some other medals. And for a long time after that, all I could eat was baby food.

"All those years, I thought about the diamonds buried in our foxhole. I was pretty sure that once the war was over, Tommy must have gone back there and dug them up and bought himself a truckload of cigarettes. In 1954, I learned he hadn't. First I started to write to the government to ask for information about him, but I didn't get any replies. Maybe because I didn't know how to spell his name or even where he had come from. Then I got a letter from somebody in one of the other platoons and he wrote that Tommy had been killed in ambush. Over time, I got more information. It seems that about three weeks before the war ended, our company was racing toward Berchtesgaden, where Hitler was supposed to be, and they walked into an ambush. Tommy and about twelve other guys were killed.

"Until the day I was wounded, I'd never had more than a few slight wounds, and neither had Tommy, and we'd been in action almost from the day we landed in France. Now, we find the diamonds, and the next thing you know, I get wounded so bad I almost die and Tommy gets killed. Let me tell you, those damn diamonds had a curse on them."

Tommy DeLion's body was sent back to his home in Morrill, Nebraska, and buried in the local cemetery (see Appendix C).

Still, no matter what else happened, Sam Nyer could not rid himself of his obsession with the diamonds, especially once he knew that Tommy had not lived to reclaim them, and that they must still be where he had buried them. He continued to dream about them, but now, unbidden, there came into his mind questions without answers: Who had owned the diamonds before? Where had they come from? How had they gotten to that room in whatever town it was? How many through the years had been cursed by them? How much blood had been spilled for them?

16

Obsession

Back home and out of the Army, Sam Nyer eventually settled in Bangor, where he started a small company selling farm tools, which managed barely to stay afloat through the years. He married a girl named Helen, and they had three sons. He never managed to put the war far behind him.

But the diamonds, now that he knew Tommy DeLion had not lived to disinter them, were never far from his mind. Someday, he kept telling himself, he would go back to that town on the Blies, though he was still convinced it must have been the Saar, back to his foxhole, its location and the landmarks burned into his memory, and reclaim his fortune, becoming rich beyond measure. "They were driving me crazy. I was dreaming about them, thinking about them, planning what I would do with them. For all I knew, those diamonds were taken from Jewish prisoners by the Nazis, so who had a claim on them? Could anybody ever trace where they came from and who they belonged to? I wanted to get them to do something with them, I don't know what. But I was sure that not searching for them would be a sin. I was sure they had to be found."

Early in the 1970s, he decided the time had come. He took his family to Europe for a vacation. On their return, he figured they would stop in France, drive out to Sarreguemines, and unearth the diamonds. "My wife was not happy about it. She kept saying something bad was sure to happen. She said the diamonds had blood on them and we should never go to find them, especially not on the Sabbath, and not where the Germans had fought battles.

"I said this was nonsense, that my son and I would go to the hill, dig up the pouch, and get away from there fast with the diamonds, and we'd be rich."

They rented a car in Paris and headed for Alsace, crossing the border into Germany at one point on the drive. Sam Nyer had never been this far into Germany before; the closest he had come was the foxhole overlooking the Blies and some scouting forays just across the border. In Germany, they saw signs dangling above the entrances to roadside inns and taverns that he was sure portended peril—a Star of David with a figure drinking from a raised stein in the center. To Sam Nyer, that figure looked like a hanging man.

"The closer we got to the French-German border, the worse I felt. My son Kenneth said it was just because I was too excited, and that I had promised him that one day we would come to the hill and dig up those diamonds, and I didn't want to disappoint him."

When they reached the border, he became disoriented. In 1945, he had approached the river from the French side. Now he was approaching from the German side and the view and the landmarks seen from this angle were hard to distinguish, and he began to realize that the river he had always thought was the Saar was actually a different one. They checked into a hotel for the night, and then, the next morning, Sam Nyer and his son started for the hill.

"I told my wife we'd be back in a couple of hours with the stones. She was very upset, but she didn't say anything. As my son and I drove out to the old battlefield, all at once I saw that where I thought there was only one hill there are, in fact, nine hills. When we got to the area as soldiers, it was nighttime, and Tommy and I never got to see the whole area. Hell, there were German land mines everywhere, and you just don't go walking around sightseeing. I studied the area and finally I thought I recognize two of the main landmarks I swore I would never forget, and they were right where they should be, so I was certain this was the right hill. So we got out of the car and started walking and memories began coming back to me, the memory of the war and the dead and the suffering, the faces of my friends, and, worst of all, the faces of the men I had killed.

"We got to the edge of the forest and I asked my son to hand me the shovel we had bought on the way. I wanted to test the ground to see if I could still dig in it after all these years.

"For the next couple of hours we dug in this foxhole and that one. We found nothing. Maybe I was wrong after all. Maybe we weren't on the right hill. Maybe it was one of the others. Or maybe somebody else had found the diamonds and taken them. But I knew one thing. The diamonds weren't for me. I was never going to find them.

"And I was sure that, as my wife said, something bad was going to happen if I did find them. Damn diamonds. I knew they were cursed."

Sam Nyer would never return to the site. He was sure the curse was hanging over him for having possessed them for even a moment. He was sure that the curse was so strong that if he tried to retrieve them, he would die. The search abandoned, Nyer and his son returned to the hotel and then headed back to Paris.

So the diamonds were left undiscovered, buried in that old foxhole in the forest on the side of one of those nine hills. It would be another fifteen years before the search resumed.

PART III

Yaron Svoray's Journey

17

A Chance for Riches

Yaron Svoray was fascinated, intrigued by Sam Nyer's tale. If Nyer refused to get on a plane bound for France, if he refused to search again for those diamonds, if he were relinquishing all claim to them, then so be it. Svoray would take up the search.

For Svoray, though, this was not some holy mission as it had never been for Nyer. He wasn't about to dig up those diamonds, obviously property stolen by the Nazis from their Jewish victims, just to turn them over to a philanthropic agency that would presumably try to track down and restore them to their rightful owners. That, he was sure, was an impossible task. The rightful owners had long ago perished in the gas chambers. No, he saw this as his chance to become wealthy for the rest of his life. His wife objected. She said, "If you find them, you have to hand them over to some sort of charity, because we have no right to make a fortune on someone else's misfortune."

He said, "Yeah, sure. I'm going to find forty diamonds and hand them over to some charity that will make them vanish faster than the blink of an eye? No way. You think I'm crazy? I'll get them, and then we'll see what we'll do." He knew precisely what he intended to do with them. The diamonds would solve all his financial problems.

And at that moment, his financial problems were enormous;

they were overwhelming him, which was not something new. All his life, whatever money he made seemed to go out faster than it came in. But then, he'd never made much anyway. Nobody makes much as a paratrooper and staff sergeant in the Israeli Army, in which he'd served for three years (from 1973 to 1976), fighting in one of Israel's bloodiest wars. And how much can someone make as a student studying political science and international affairs at Hebrew University in Jerusalem (from 1976 to 1977), or as a detective in Yamar, the Israeli equivalent of the FBI (from 1979 to 1983) or as a lecturer on international terrorism (since 1983)? When he met Sam Nyer in the middle of 1988, he was in the United States working toward a master's degree in film studies and communications at Queens College in New York, trying to support his wife, Mikhal, and a growing family, on whatever he could eke out doing a thousand odd jobs, from chauffeuring for Leona Helmsley, to working as a correspondent for *Hadashot,* an Israeli daily newspaper, to traveling around the United States giving lectures on Middle Eastern politics and terrorism drawn from his experiences as a detective and an international investigator.

So Nyer's story, Svoray thought, far-fetched as it seemed, might be a way out of the abyss of debt and poverty.

He had no idea at that time what lay ahead; he had no way of knowing that he was about to set out on a journey that would last eleven years, years filled with detours and perils, that would lead him into the heart of the neo-Nazi movement in Germany as an agent for the Simon Wiesenthal Center, that would send him into the sickening depths of the pornographic "snuff" film business worldwide, that would steer him into a vast international counterfeiting operation whose origins lay in the Nazi death camps.

It was not until 1996, at Yad Vashem, the Holocaust memorial in Jerusalem, that he finally saw what, perhaps, he should have known from the beginning, should have seen every step of the way, through every diversion. Looming over everything, the pivot on which everything turned, was the Holocaust. It was the glue that bound it all together. No matter where he looked, no matter what detours he took, the seemingly unrelated roads he traveled were all interconnected with echoes of the "Final Solution." Without the Holocaust, the concentration camps, there would have been no diamonds for Sam Nyer and Tommy DeLion to "liberate" and then bury. There would have been no Nazi loot at all.

But it was a decade before he realized that. At the start, and for a long time afterward, knowing all that Sam Nyer had told him, he was as obsessed with the diamonds as Nyer had been, feeling that uncovering them for his own profit was now his life's work.

18

Persuasion

After his first encounter with Nyer following that lecture in Bangor, Svoray spent the next two weeks compiling a long list of questions. They had to be answered. The first one, of course, was, Is this guy Nyer a nutcase? He asked people in the Jewish organizations that were sponsoring his lectures, a friend who knew people in Bangor, and a lot of others. The unanimous response was this: Nyer is a solid citizen. When he mentioned the story about the diamonds, people laughed. "He's told that story a thousand times," Svoray was told. "Every time he shows up at a veterans' meeting, he starts on it. People see him and they say, 'Here he comes again with that bullshit story about buried treasure.'"

Maybe nobody else believed him, but Svoray figured he had nothing to lose, and everything to gain, by trying to follow up on the tale to see if it panned out. Two weeks after their first meeting, Svoray called Nyer and asked for second meeting. "I have a hundred questions I want to ask you."

Nyer agreed. For the next two days, at his house, with his wife sometimes sitting in the corner staring at both of them with a suspicious look and interrupting Nyer constantly, and at times in a delicatessen on the main street in Bangor where the pastrami and corned beef were terrible, Svoray put those hundred questions to him. Nyer answered them all. He had an incredible memory, especially for the things that happened during the war. He gave Svoray the names and addresses, as many as he knew, of his old Army buddies, finding even more among papers tucked away in various places.

But everything kept coming around to the one thing that Svoray really wanted to know. How could Nyer not go back and pick up those stones? How could Nyer simply leave them there all these years, buried in that foxhole? Svoray was sure that if he had been in Nyer's shoes, he'd have crawled over broken glass to get them.

At their next meeting, he jokingly said that to Nyer, who immediately grew irritated and cagey. The good feelings that Svoray thought had begun to develop between them vanished. "The diamonds are cursed," Nyer said, "and I want nothing to do with them."

But Svoray wasn't listening. He'd stopped listening as soon as Nyer went into his litany about curses. Svoray grew belligerent. What the hell, he told himself, if Nyer hasn't got the nerve to go after them, then screw him. All Svoray needed was to raise some cash and he'd be on his way by himself. He was sure it wouldn't be hard to find the diamonds. In fact, he was already mulling over ways to sell the diamonds when he had them in his hands. He'd simply take them to Ramat Gan, the diamond district in Israel, or to Amsterdam, and he'd dispose of them in such a way that he wouldn't be hounded for the rest of his life by Internal Revenue Service agents.

But then he realized that such thoughts and plans weren't getting him any closer to his goal. If he were going to search for the gems, he'd need every detail he could acquire. So he calmed himself down, placated Nyer, told him he understood how Nyer felt, and then asked for as many details as possible about the location of the hill and the foxhole.

It worked. They became friends again. Nyer explained the topography of the region, and then hovered over Svoray when the Israeli tried to sketch out the area, making corrections, adding a detail here and there.

As for the contention that the diamonds were cursed, Svoray decided to keep his mouth shut, even though to him that notion seemed ludicrous and childish. The diamonds were there, waiting for someone to find them and use them as he would. Svoray was going to be that someone.

What Nyer wouldn't do was participate or put a nickel into the hunt. "If I do," he said, "something bad will happen to me and my family. I told you, I keep telling you, those diamonds are cursed. They're not meant for me. They've already nearly cost me my life, twice."

"If they're cursed," Svoray said, "what about me?"

"If you want to search for them, that's your problem," he said.

"Then why did you tell me all this?"

Nyer shrugged. "I was simply telling you a story. If you want to do something about it, that's your business."

It was frustrating. Svoray began to wonder if this was all a pipe dream, just something Nyer had made up out of whole cloth, and he was falling for it. And then something happened that persuaded him that Nyer was telling the absolute truth. It was the sudden appearance in the room of Nyer's wife. She walked in during the middle of their conversation, glared at Svoray, glared at her husband, and started yelling at him, berating him, scorning him, treating him like a child, Syoray thought. He cowered. At that instant Svoray was overwhelmed with the sense that the last thing Sam Nyer would ever do was lie to this woman. He had schlepped her to Europe, to Germany of all places, on that aborted trip to find the diamonds. He never would have done such a thing, never would have told her his story of the buried diamonds in the first place, if he hadn't buried them and if he wasn't sure they were still there. If it had been a wild-goose chase, if it had all been a lie, she never would have let him forget it. It would have haunted him for the rest of his life, leaving him without a moment's peace. From that day on, whenever people asked Svoray why he ever believed the story, his reply was always, "You never met his wife. He might have lied to everyone else, but not to her. He wouldn't have dared."

A few hours later, he was on his way back to New York. He knew three things. Sam Nyer had told the truth. Svoray was going to get those diamonds and become rich. And at that moment, he had no idea how he was going to do it.

19

To Alsace

For the next five months, he tried every way he could to raise enough money to get to France, travel to Alsace, and figure out which hill overlooking the Saar was the right one. Then he was sure he'd be able to dig up the diamonds in a matter of hours. During the day, he studied at the university and filed stories for the newspaper back in Israel. Once or twice a week, he flew out of New York to give lectures for Israeli bonds or the United Jewish Appeal, rushing to make planes in and out of La Guardia, sometimes returning just in time to make his next class.

And he spent his spare time studying diamonds, learning as much about them as he could. He had absolutely no interest in their historical background, where they had come from or who had owned them before. He was interested only in learning enough so that when he finally had them, he'd have some idea of how much they were worth.

He bought maps of France, especially of Alsace, of the French-German border area. He concentrated on the city of Sarreguemines. Nyer may not have been exactly certain which of the nine hills contained the foxhole in which he and Tommy DeLion had buried the diamonds. He may not have been certain of its precise location in relation to the German-French border. He may not have even been certain which river he looked across from his foxhole, though he thought it was probably the Saar. But he did remember Sarreguemines, remembered marching through it the first night on the way to the hill, and he had a memory of seeing a sign with its name on it as he lay on the stretcher at the evacuation center, waiting to die.

Svoray could concentrate on little else but Sam Nyer's story. It was not only dominating his life, it was beginning to affect his marriage. His wife, Mikhal, was not happy living in America in the first place, especially in the poorest section of Flushing, Queens, trying to feed, clothe, and raise two young children practically alone, her husband away fourteen or more hours every day. She had sacrificed a career as a respected and talented jewelry designer in Israel to follow him to New York so he could finish his studies. While she rarely complained, there were signs of her unhappiness; she adamantly refused to consider either of them getting a Green Card or applying for United States citizenship, though they had the opportunity. Israel was her home, and that was where she wished to return, where she wished to spend her life.

Now she was inundated with stories about the diamonds. Svoray kept telling her that he was going to find them and, when he did, their lives were going to change drastically. Who knew how much those forty stones were worth; but he was sure they'd bring at least enough so that they could have homes in both the United States and Israel, and that they'd be rich enough to do whatever they wanted.

She was skeptical. "Even if what this man says is a thousand percent true," she said, "there's almost no chance that you'll ever be able to find that one single hole in the ground."

"I'll find it," Svoray kept insisting.

"How can you be willing to spend thousands of dollars, which we don't have, on a story you heard from a man you don't know?"

"I'll get the money and I'll find the stones."

In all their years of marriage, they had barely had a handful of major arguments. But over this a storm was brewing, on the verge of erupting.

And then it seemed his luck was about to change. His brother, Ori, who lived in Australia, called to say he was on his way to Europe for a vacation. They had not seen each other in three years, and he asked if it was possible for Svoray to join him. Not only did Svoray agree, even if it took his last penny, but he told his brother the story of the diamonds and asked if he'd like to join an excursion, find the hill, and dig them up.

Ori Svoray laughed. Not for a minute did he believe the story, believe in the hill, but he saw this as a good opportunity for the brothers to get together again after so long. So he agreed.

Mikhal didn't argue. After all, how could she stand in the way of two brothers seeing each other after a long separation?

In August of 1988, the brothers made their way to Alsace, to the French-German border. As soon as they saw the sign pointing to Sarreguemines, they stopped the car. Yaron pulled out his notes, diagrams, and maps, and studied them. He figured the best thing to do was go into the town and then start walking along the same route Sam Nyer had followed. He had said that the walk from town to the hill and the foxhole had taken two or three hours. But he and his company had been burdened with all their equipment and were forced to be careful. After all, they were faced with crossing minefields, and they had to be watchful for enemy soldiers who might be waiting in ambush anywhere. What had taken him three hours, Svoray figured, ought to take them a lot less time. So, he planned to walk about two hours; by then they should be in the right place.

About midday, Yaron started walking. Ori drove the car

slowly behind him. Yaron was absolutely amazed by Sam Nyer's memory, and his ability to recall even the smallest detail. There was the church with the kneeling statue of the Virgin Mary at the crossroads, and there were other landmarks Nyer had mentioned. But, as they left the outskirts of the city, his certainty began to fade. Less than a mile up the road, there were several fields. Behind them, there appeared what seemed to be a long, continuous line of hills. Svoray walked into the nearest field and kept looking at the diagrams, trying to follow the instructions. Farmers passed by, giving him hardly a glance. Finally, he ended up in a thick forest overlooking several villages, and his spirits went soaring when he noticed several foxholes and trenches dug into the ground.

He waved to Ori, who stopped the car. "This is the place," Yaron told him. "We're at the right hill."

"You're sure?" Ori asked.

"Absolutely," Yaron said. He could hardly believe it. It hadn't taken him days, only hours, to reach what he was sure was the right place, to come very close to Sam Nyer's foxhole and the diamonds. When Yaron had pressed Nyer about details, he had been absolutely certain. So Yaron had devised a system to locate the particular foxhole by triangulating from one place to all the things Nyer had seen—the church steeple, the wooden bridge, the burnt-out farmhouse, the river, the town or outskirts of the city, the downward slope, and all the rest. Now Yaron was standing near a foxhole and he could see those landmarks. This had to be the place.

What he didn't realize then was that there were foxholes and church steeples and farmhouses and bridges and rivers and settlements and fields and slopes all over the area, and depending on where you happened to be, you could almost always triangulate and see them. And they weren't necessarily the right ones. What he didn't fully comprehend, or perhaps wasn't willing to accept just then, was that hills and ridges have two sides, and even if you find the right hill, you could be on the wrong side of it. Still, at that moment, he didn't consider any of that, so convinced was he that this was the right hill and the right place.

His brother was not so sure. He was a pilot, and he suggested that there seemed to be a lot of hills covered with forests just like the one on which they were standing, and probably all of them had foxholes and trenches, since the French had been dug in around this area in 1914 and again in 1939 to ward off impending German invasions. Maybe, he said, they ought to rent a plane and fly over to survey the whole region and make sure.

Yaron told him there was no need. *He* was sure this was the place. The problem at that moment, he said, was that they had neglected to bring along any equipment to dig into the foxholes. They would have to go and buy or rent some shovels and picks and the rest and then return and begin to dig.

But first Yaron wanted to do a little digging with his bare hands. Maybe he'd be lucky and there the diamonds would be. He fell to his knees in one of the foxholes that seemed to fit Nyer's description and started to dig into the muddy soil. A half-hour later, he'd found nothing, was covered with mud, and realized that they really did need tools.

They went back to the car and started driving, not to Sarreguemines but toward Germany. Yaron figured that once they crossed the border and looked back, they'd see what Nyer had seen when he had returned and was sure he had spotted his hill on the day he collapsed with a heart attack in the early 1970s. At this point, before the European Union became a reality, there were borders with border guards checking passports and visas and asking questions. You couldn't just drive straight through from one country to another without a worry or a question or a guard to stop you. So, when the Svoray brothers reached the border, there was the gatehouse and there was a guard who ordered them to stop and show their papers and passports. The guard studied them carefully. Yaron didn't realize then that the reason the guard was so careful was that this was a well-known border crossing for smugglers. The guard looked surprised and uncertain when he saw the Israeli passport.

After a moment's hesitation, he handed the passports back and waved them through. Once in Germany, they stopped, and Yaron stared back. What he saw was not one forest-covered hill but the nine hills covered with forests that Sam Nyer had seen the day of his return. Yaron's heart sank. But he drove on, into Saarbrücken, the nearest big city, bought shovels and picks, and then drove back. Two hours later, they were on the hill. Until nightfall, they dug and found nothing. Yaron was certain they must be close to the right foxhole; it was the carrot dangling at the end of the stick. Maybe it was there, but he didn't find it.

In Sarreguemines, they checked into the Hôtel Alsace. The clerk didn't look happy to see two mud-covered men carrying picks and shovels. Still, he gave them a room. He also called the police, because at one in the morning the gendarmes came knocking at the door and rushed into the room when it opened. Yaron Svoray remembers that they acted as though they were convinced they were about to apprehend two major criminals. Actually, as he learned later, all they wanted was to find out what these two mud-covered strangers were doing wandering around the countryside.

Then Yaron made matters worse. The brothers were covered with mud, so they must have looked suspicious. Yaron didn't speak French, and he and Ori were obviously not locals, which meant they were automatically under a cloud. And the gendarmes didn't speak English or Hebrew. Yaron grew agitated, and began to shout at them, treating them as though they were third-world bumpkins. Later, looking back on the scene, he was sure they would probably have ended up in the local jail if Ori hadn't come to the rescue. Fortunately, he spoke enough French to persuade them that Yaron was a journalist, though he didn't explain what a journalist might be doing in their territory. They took down the details, though the way they kept looking at Yaron convinced him that he had just made himself the number-one enemy of the Sarreguemines police force.

From that day on, he was sure he was a marked man. It seemed as though somebody was watching his every move. If he'd only kept his cool and not exploded, things might have gone easier and nobody would have bothered them. But, as it was, things got very complicated. The local gendarmes alerted the local forest ranger, Pierre Le Grande, a tough, old, retired, professional soldier with an unruly, gray-streaked beard, hard brown eyes, and a tight mouth, who looked like an old-time highway robber out of some local legend. He didn't like strangers in his forest. So the Svoray brothers were forced to play a complicated game of hide-and-seek, sneaking into the forest and digging for short intervals until Le Grande showed up and ordered them out.

The next six days were a reprise. They'd head into the forest, make sure nobody was watching, find a likely foxhole, dig for perhaps thirty minutes, find nothing, move on to the next, find nothing, and then Le Grande would show up and throw them out.

By the end of the week, the money was running out, and it was more and more obvious that this game with Le Grande and the local cops was about as stupid as could be. Yaron was sure that if he happened to cross their invisible line in the sand, he'd find himself in the Sarreguemines jail on a charge he would not understand; but they'd find a charge and make it stick. He seemed on the verge of making himself persona non grata in

that part of Alsace, and if that happened, his search would come
to an abrupt end and he would never be able to resume it.

At the end of that week they headed back to Paris, out of
money and, it seemed, no closer to finding Sam Nyer's foxhole
and the diamonds than when they had started. Yaron knew that
he'd have to come up with enough money to return, and when
he did, he'd make peace with the locals and find the diamonds.

20

Finding a Friend

Back in New York, as Svoray contemplated the events that had occurred in Alsace, he understood that he was faced with a major problem. He hated the French. He hated what seemed to him their condescension toward all foreigners. He hated their lack of interest in speaking any language but their own, and their refusal to communicate with strangers. He saw them as his enemies, the ones he would have to outsmart, defeat. It was as simple as that. Such an attitude, he realized, was going to be a major roadblock preventing him from reaching his goal.

That goal, returning to Alsace and unearthing the diamonds, dominated every waking moment of his life. Nothing else seemed important but those riches waiting in the foxhole in the forest. Whatever problems he was having—in school, at home, with his family, with money—evaporated in his dreams of becoming rich beyond measure.

He not only dreamed about it, he talked about it to just about everybody he met, and everybody thought he was crazy. He became convinced that as soon as he left the room, people began laughing at him and his quest. If they didn't think he was simply stupid, they were sure he was naïve, misguided at the very least. Some would even call Mikhal and commiserate with her.

He tried to ignore the whispers and the pitying looks, concentrating instead on trying to amass enough money for a second trip to the hill. He gave little thought to the implications of this whole quest. He had only a cursory knowledge about the war, and almost no knowledge, except for what Nyer had told him, about the battles in Alsace on the border between France and Germany. And at that moment he didn't bother to dig deeper. He wasn't concerned then about the origin of the diamonds, where they had come from to reach the foxhole, or what they might have cost to those who had owned them, not just in money but in blood and lives.

In fact, he had only a rudimentary knowledge about the Holocaust, though he was the son of parents who had escaped the worst, and many relatives whom he never knew had perished in the Nazi death camps. His grandfather, Carl Sobersky, a bemedaled veteran of the German Army in World War I, owner of Heinrich Sobersky & Son, a prosperous sales representative for many German clothing manufacturers, fled his native Berlin in 1938 for Palestine with Svoray's grandmother and his father, then named Heinz Yehuda Sobersky, who dropped the Heinz later (Svoray's Aunt Lily was sent to England some months earlier). He left behind all his wealth, all his possessions, everything the family had worked to achieve over decades. And he left behind, too, relatives who did not survive. The name Svoray was not adopted until after the war when many Israelis, in the flush of independence, were shedding their European backgrounds and taking on new, Jewish names.

Svoray's mother, born Rachel Stern in Egypt, was taken by her family to Romania while she was still a child, and saw most of her relatives perish in the extermination camps when the Nazis conquered Romania and began the mass killing of Jews there. In 1943, she, her father and mother, and a few other relatives, all still holding Egyptian citizenship, managed with those passports to reach safety, finally to reach the Holy Land. Those left behind disappeared forever.

Yet Svoray really knew little about all that had happened, not merely to his family but to all the other millions. He knew only what most people knew, not the details, not the depths.

In the months that followed his first trip to Alsace, he squirreled away enough money to make a second trip around Christmas of 1988. He stayed a week, returned home, and then made a third trip at the end of January 1989. On both trips, he made his way directly to the hill and dug in the soil of every foxhole he found. The digging was much harder now that it was winter and the ground was frozen. It was like digging into cement. He kept a constant eye out for Le Grande, trying to dodge him, and dug frantically. He found nothing. He returned home, frustrated, but convinced that, given time, eventually he would zero in on the right place and emerge a rich man.

Then Jonathan Bucksbaum seemed to provide an answer. A thin, dark-eyed, cool, sardonic, trim man in his early forties with a perfect command of French, he was one of Svoray's professors in film studies. Svoray was certainly not his best student, but because he was in his late thirties—considerably older than the twenty-year-olds who filled the class—he was, perhaps, more focused, with his insatiable thirst for films. One day, Bucksbaum showed the class Alain Resnais's short documentary, *Night and Fog*, a juxtaposition of scenes from the concentration camps across Germany and Poland with present-day denials of the Holocaust. It had a powerful impact on the whole class—on the students who had never seen a Holocaust film before, on those who knew only its outlines, and especially on

Svoray. It was his first link between the diamonds and the destruction of the European Jews. But it was a vague one, the implications not yet reaching the front of his mind.

Then he had an idea. Jonathan Bucksbaum spoke French and knew France, spending his vacations there traveling the countryside on an old Norton motorbike and teaching courses on American films. Jonathan Bucksbaum was absorbed in the Holocaust, and since Svoray had begun to see a tie between the Holocaust and the diamonds, perhaps he could entice his professor to join the hunt. Svoray made an appointment to see Bucksbaum after class, sat in his office, and told him Sam Nyer's story. Bucksbaum was amused, but Svoray's enthusiasm was infectious, and before long Bucksbaum agreed to go along and act as translator and guide into the soul and persona of the French, just as long as it didn't interfere with his scheduled plans.

Now the problem was getting enough money to make the trip. It was soon after the bombing of Pan Am 103 over Lockerbie, Scotland, and Svoray was gaining a reputation as a lecturer on the complex problems of terrorism and the Middle East. During one of those lectures for Israeli bonds in a small Midwestern city, he met a man who was fascinated by the talk, and he invited Svoray to dine with him and his wife. During the meal, Svoray told him Sam Nyer's story and how he, Svoray, was trying to raise the money to resume the search for the diamonds. This man was very rich and he was bored with his life, but bound to his city by business. After listening to the saga, he offered to finance a trip. How would Svoray repay him? "Don't worry about it," he said. "If you find the diamonds, just pay me back what I'm giving you. I don't need to make a profit. I'll think of this as an interesting way to use some of my money."

This was a one-time venture on his part. He was not the last person to advance Svoray funds to pursue the dream. Through the years, a number of others did the same, some with the idea that if Svoray found the diamonds, they would get a share of the profits, others with no thought of profit but merely because they believed it was a search worth making and they wanted to help. They would advance the money once, and that would be it. If Svoray were successful, they would be repaid. If he failed, then it was just an investment on their part that didn't pan out, and they would absorb the loss. They could afford to.

Svoray arrived back in New York after this lecture with enough money to pay his way to France with Jonathan Bucksbaum. From Paris, they headed for Alsace, for Sarreguemines. Bucksbaum, Svoray hoped, would be able to assuage some of the ill feelings he had left behind.

They tracked down the local archivist at the city hall. With Bucksbaum translating (and smoothing over some of Svoray's brusqueness), Svoray asked questions about the area as it was during the war, hoping to get an exact fix on Nyer's location, on his hill. The answers were a shock. On three different sides of Sarreguemines there were hills on which the Americans had been dug in during the war, and every one of those hills looked down on the Saar, the Blies, or one of their tributaries. Fierce battles had been fought all over the area, on all those hills, in Forbach and all the other towns and villages, which, forty years later, had become suburbs of the ever-expanding Sarreguemines.

The prospect was anything but enticing. Was Svoray now going to have to search not merely the nine hills that Nyer had seen on his return but all the others as well? Svoray was sure that, following the directions Nyer had given him and his impressions of the area and its landmarks, he knew the right hill and shouldn't bother with all those others. Bucksbaum was not as convinced. He was more open, more willing to explore, and so for the next two days they crisscrossed the terrain, in and out of forests, up and down hills, back and forth across the border.

When they reached one of the hills close to Forbach, Svoray was stunned. There were dozens, scores, of foxholes, just as there were on the other hills. And from this hill, it was possible to triangulate and see all the landmarks that perfectly fit Nyer's description.

So now they would have to explore this hill further. But first, Svoray decided to do some more digging in the original hill. When they reached it, his nemesis, Forest Ranger Le Grande, was waiting, with his hard, round, gendarme cap and his large shotgun nestled on his left shoulder. He glared and blocked the way. Svoray and Bucksbaum tried to reason with him, Bucksbaum trying to calm Svoray's mounting rage. Le Grande would have none of it. Svoray offered him a bribe (something local officials, cops, mayors, and party bureaucrats generally accepted with alacrity, suddenly becoming at least partly cooperative). He looked furious at the suggestion. He was old school, honest in his way, loyal to his masters—German and Vichy during the war, French Republic now—to whatever government was in power, incorruptible by his lights.

Svoray was hard put to understand his attitude. After all, these hills, these forests were public lands, not private property. Local citizens and tourists from all over used them for hiking, picnicking, camping. But Le Grande didn't want the two of them, or most particularly Svoray, wandering through what he considered his private preserve. It wasn't just that he had taken an instant dislike to Svoray; he must have sensed that the Israeli was not just an innocent tourist exploring his forests, but someone with other, darker motives.

Every time they returned to the hill, Le Grande was waiting, blocking their way. On the third day, he had company—local cops. Svoray tried to explain to them that he was not there to make trouble, and besides, he was a fellow cop back home (a small lie, though true in the past). They stonewalled. Svoray was not at that moment projecting the attitude of "You anti-Semitic bastards are persecuting me, a poor Jew," though he was getting close. Instead he put on a show of indignation and chutzpah, which got their backs up. They not only ordered Svoray and Bucksbaum off the hill, but they escorted them back to the car and stood there until they drove away.

That evening, trying to plan his next step, trying to figure out a way to circumvent Le Grande and the gendarmes, Svoray wandered aimlessly along the banks of the Blies River. Sitting on a small stool in the middle of the path that ran alongside the river was a huge, white-haired man wearing a large straw hat, corduroy pants, and a checkered shirt buttoned to the neck, a thin cigarette dangling from his mouth, a fishing pole held loosely in his hands. He looked to be in his late seventies or eighties. He seemed half asleep. There was no way to get by him; on the right was the river, on the left a steep embankment. The old man opened his eyes and looked up as Svoray stopped in front of him. Svoray greeted him in English, asking if he could pass by. The old man smiled, shrugged his shoulders, and indicated that he did not speak or understand English. There was, though, something appealing, endearing about him, and Svoray took an instantaneous liking to him. Svoray needed a friend, someone who lived in the area who might help him. Perhaps he had found one.

Stiffly, with great difficulty, the old man tried to get up from the stool, seeming as though his whole body had frozen in place after a long rest in one position. Svoray reached out and helped him to his feet. The man murmured thanks and stood there, dangling his fishing pole and line into the river. Instead of going on, Svoray remained and watched him fish. He said something in French; Svoray replied in English; and the only way they understood each other was with hand signals and nods of the head. The old man's name was Marcel Pierron.

Then a young blond man showed up. He was Pierron's grandson, and he had arrived to escort his grandfather home. The grandson spoke English and translated Pierron's sudden invitation for Svoray to join him at his home for dinner. Svoray explained that he had a friend waiting for him at the hotel in Sarreguemines. The friend should come along, Pierron said. And detailed directions were given.

At the hotel, Bucksbaum was playing chess with the owner. Svoray pried him loose, and a short time later they followed the directions to the Pierron homestead. When they were driving down the gravel path, it became apparent that Marcel Pierron was not a simple, elderly fisherman whiling away his retirement years. The house, hidden behind well-tended trees, gardens, and lawns, was huge. A maid opened the front door and led them into a large study. Pierron greeted them warmly and offered them drinks. Svoray explained that he didn't drink alcohol. Bucksbaum did drink and accepted, and Pierron uncorked a bottle of vintage wine with a very familiar, and expensive, label. Over the next several hours, he and Bucksbaum finished that bottle and opened another, and they dined on a meal that made Svoray understand why the French have such a well-deserved reputation for good food. And they talked and talked and talked.

Pierron's roots in this region of Alsace went back generations. His father had owned a small bookstore and, after the war, Marcel Pierron had turned it into one of the largest schoolbook-printing companies in Alsace and one of the area's largest and most respected employers. During the German occupation, he had worked with the French underground, the Maquis, his position in the community giving him a certain degree of latitude. During the first years of the occupation, he said, the Germans had seemed friendly and even benevolent, unless you happened to be a Jew. But as the war turned against them, they became brutal, vindictive, and hostile, rounding up civilians as hostages, imposing strict curfews, shooting on sight those out after hours. It was a bad time, and Pierron's situation, as an ally of the resistance, even if a clandestine one, was often perilous.

As the evening wore on, Pierron asked what Svoray and Bucksbaum were doing in the area. He assumed that both were Americans. Svoray did not challenge the assumption, did not say that he was actually Jewish, an Israeli, uncertain what reaction such a disclosure might bring, given that the anti-Semitism that had been so prevalent in this region in the past had not fully vanished in the present. Pierron pressed for more details. Svoray became guarded, said something about loving historical sights, about an interest in wars, and a lot of other nonsense. Pierron's eyes crinkled with amusement. He wasn't buying any of it.

"I know why you are here," he said just before they left.

Svoray's heart sank. He was sure Pierron was going to say that he, or someone he knew, had unearthed the diamonds years before, sold them, and was living on the profits. Svoray felt sick. Had all his efforts been in vain, all his dreams, a chimera?

Pierron put his hand on Svoray's shoulder and said, "I know you are here to find out about those missing soldiers."

Svoray's relief was palpable. He took a deep breath of relief, the air expelled from his lungs. Pierron was not talking about the diamonds. As for the missing soldiers, Sam Nyer had mentioned Sergeant Wolfe and his unit, but Svoray had not paid much attention at the time. It didn't seem very important, didn't seem like anything that would help him in his search. Now Pierron was mentioning it. Maybe it meant something after all. Svoray decided to be interested, feeling he had nothing to lose and, in expressing interest in what Pierron had to say, everything to gain by ingratiating himself with this new friend. Svoray nodded. "Yes, you've got it. That's why we're here, to find out about what happened to those soldiers. How did you figure that out?"

Pierron smiled. "Listen, we have had three different American investigating teams here in this town since 1945 looking for those twelve American soldiers. I imagine they were everywhere in the region. I told all of them when they came to me that I had no idea what happened to them or what they did. But it is interesting, isn't it?"

"Yes, very interesting," Svoray agreed. An idea began churning in his mind. He didn't know what to do with it then, but he was sure he had just been handed some very valuable information, especially since it was a story that had been bruited about for nearly half a century. It was just a hunch, but Svoray had spent his adult life acting on hunches, and they'd paid off more often than not.

As they drove away from Pierron's home, Svoray said to Bucksbaum, "That story of the missing American soldiers is going to get me my diamonds. I feel it in my bones. I know it."

As soon as they were back at the hotel, he placed a call to Sam Nyer. Did Nyer remember talking about the missing American soldiers?

Nyer's memory, usually so complete and precise, failed him this time. Before Svoray could ask more, his phone card ran out of time, and he could not get another one until morning. Just before they were disconnected, Svoray asked Nyer to think hard, try to remember, and Svoray would be back in touch very soon.

Bucksbaum was waiting when Svoray got back to the room. He didn't look happy. They had been asked to visit the local gendarmes the next morning.

Why?

He didn't know, but the summons was not issued lightly, not something that could be ignored.

At police headquarters the following morning, they were met by a stern-faced sergeant. They had been, he declared, trespassing on private property. He had been getting many complaints. The implication was clear. They had better stop what they were doing. If he kept getting more complaints, they were going to wind up in his jail.

Furious, Svoray demanded to know whose property they were trespassing on, and where the laws were that said a tourist couldn't roam through forests that were public property.

The sergeant grew increasingly belligerent. Every time they crossed a field on their way to another hill, he declared, they were trespassing on some farmer's private property. As for the forests being public, they were public for local residents and not for every outsider who came from who knew where. Then he demanded to know what they were really doing in the area.

It had something to do with the war, Svoray stuttered, sounding unconvincing, even to himself. Some of his relatives had fought in the area and he was looking for signs of the battle. He was sure they were free to go wherever they wanted. That was the right of everyone, not just local people.

It went on and on without being resolved, and by the time they left police headquarters, Svoray knew one thing for sure. He would need a very good cover story if he were going to continue, because without one, he would not be able to move a step in the region. Even if he didn't end up in jail, his search would come to a sudden halt.

So another journey to the hill came to an end. Svoray was out of money again; everything he had put away, everything that had been lent to him—all gone. What had begun, in some ways, as a lark, as a kind of exciting adventure with profit at the end, was turning into a disaster. The expenses were mounting, debts, accumulating, and a happy end was nowhere in sight. He began to wonder if Sam Nyer were right that the diamonds were, indeed, cursed, and anyone who sought them, doomed.

But two things stood out, told him that there was still hope. He had made a friend who could aid him in the future. And he had found a story that might provide a cloak for his real purpose. He would use that story, elaborate on it, set the disappearance of the missing dozen not somewhere to the South, but in the hills and forests of this part of Alsace.

Yaron Svoray during the filming of the *Blood from a Stone* documentary in the Library of Innsbruck. (Scott Duncan)

Yaron Svoray spent eleven years scouring the hills and forests
of Alsace in search of one foxhole among thousands, trying to find
the Life Diamonds. (Scott Duncan)

Rough-cut diamonds. (Scott Duncan)

Yaron Svoray and Rick Kaufman. (Scott Duncan)

Rick Kaufman, Canadian entrepreneur, joined the search party at the last minute. His job: if the diamonds were found, take them and guide them on a new journey to redemption. (Scott Duncan)

Ako Hintzen, German intelligence expert, was in charge of security during the final search for the foxhole. He and his men were armed against any impending danger. (Scott Duncan)

For a half century after he and Tommy DeLion liberated and then buried the Life Diamonds, Sam Nyer's life has been shadowed by the curse that surrounded them. (Scott Duncan)

While a prisoner at KZ Vught, Jacques Firth, an Amsterdam diamond expert, waited in vain for the Nazis to supply him with the diamonds they looted from all over occupied Europe. (The History Channel)

KZ Vught, the only offically designated concentration camp in the Netherlands. (The History Channel)

Ako Hintzen and Yaron Svoray. (The History Channel)

Alan Kannof, COO, William Morris Agency,
New York Office. (The History Channel)

Tommy DeLion's survivors gather in Ulysses, Kansas, in the spring of 2002, to hear Sam Nyer and Yaron Svoray tell of his war and his death. (Scott Duncan)

On his final leave, Tommy DeLion gave this photo to his family. This was the last time they ever saw him. Today the photo rests on a mantel in the family home in Kansas and has been an inspiration to his descendants. (Scott Duncan)

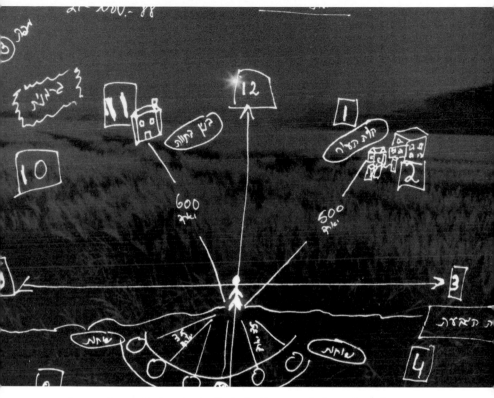

In an attempt to locate the foxhole, Svoray tried to triangulate
the landmarks seen by Sam Nyer. He didn't then realize
that the same landmarks could be seen from many hills
in many directions. (The History Channel)

Looking over the Blies River. In the winter of 1945, the German Army was entrenched in the town and the hills beyond. (Richard Hammer)

Richard Hammer and Mel Berger prepare to enter the forest in search of Sam Nyer's foxhole. Neither realized at the time the crucial role each would play over the next hours.

A foxhole in a forest on the hill, in Alsace. On this July day in 1999,
the group digs, hoping to uncover the buried diamonds.

Rick Kaufman digs through the mud of the foxhole in search of the buried diamonds. (Richard Hammer)

The lost is found. The first of the forty buried Life Diamonds emerges from the foxhole in Alsace. (Mel Berger)

21

The Missing Dozen

It was a disconsolate return to New York for Svoray. He had to face Mikhal and tell her that the diamonds still eluded his attempts to find them, that they were not about to get out of Flushing soon, that actually they were in a deeper financial hole than ever. He tried to convince her that he would find a way out, but she just gave him a look that said she didn't believe him. He tried to get back into a routine that would at least keep them afloat, studying, writing as much as possible for his Israeli newspaper, flying around the country lecturing. In time he would reach out to Sam Nyer and learn more about those missing soldiers, convinced that this would be the necessary cover story when he next returned to Alsace. He was sure it would not do to merely talk to Nyer on the phone. It would have to be face to face, where he could probe and watch Nyer's reactions.

But it was months before a lecture date took him back to Bangor. Once there, he reached out to Nyer, and that evening they sat again in the old soldier's den. Svoray was neither as friendly nor warm as he had been in the past. He was even a little hostile, resentful, feeling that Nyer had suckered him into a trap from which there was no escape.

Nyer seemed to enjoy Svoray's discomfort, laughing at the tale of the misadventures with Forest Ranger Le Grande, of the continuing failed attempts to find the foxhole, perhaps even the right forest. But when Svoray mentioned Marcel Pierron and asked again if Nyer remembered talking about the missing soldiers, Nyer grinned and nodded. It had come back to him the more he thought about it, he said. He was getting old, his memory not all it had once been—now clear and sharp sometimes, foggy at other times—and, with his heart condition, he was not in the best physical shape, seeming even a little frailer than when they had first met. He proceeded to relate his memories of Sergeant Wolfe and his twelve-man squad.

"Until I met him," Nyer said, "I thought I was the only Jew on the front lines. Then he turned up, an older guy, maybe in his thirties. We didn't become friends right away, but we used to see each other from time to time, and he'd lecture me about what was happening to the Jews in Germany and the rest of Europe, and how even our army was filled with anti-Semites. I hadn't thought much about that before. I saw him now and then, and then we kind of lost touch until sometime in early January 1945, I think it was, when one night he just showed up out of nowhere at my foxhole. He seemed very tired and like he'd aged a dozen years since the last time. He told me he wanted to talk to me, alone. He proceeded to tell me he was going to take his squad and get out before the attack on the German Fatherland began.

"He said, 'I'm not going to have my boys die. We've come this far and I haven't lost one man, and I'm not going to lose any now.'

"He was talking about desertion, which could mean a firing squad, or certainly a very long time in prison. He said, 'I want you to come along with us.'

"I said, 'Why me?'

"He said, 'Because you're a Jew in the first place, the only other Jew beside me in the whole fucking Army. And you're a scout, so you can find us the best way out of here.'

"I told him to forget about it, go get some rest, and he'd see reason the next morning. He shook his head, shook my hand, and said he was determined to do it and he'd look me up one day after the war was over.

"I didn't think about him or what he'd said until a few days later when two officers, all neat and polished from behind the lines, showed up and started asking questions about Wolfe and his men, about how they were missing and nobody knew what had happened to them. Somebody must have remembered that Wolfe was a Jew and I was a Jew, and figured Jews stick together so maybe I knew something. These two guys come to me, and they start being condescending and making anti-Semitic remarks, and I told them to get lost, that I didn't know anything.

"For a couple of days, Wolfe and his men were on everybody's tongues, people saying they'd gone into Germany on a secret mission, or they'd deserted to Switzerland or Paris or somewhere, and then the subject just died.

"You know something," Nyer said almost as an afterthought, "I think, in fact I'm sure of it, I saw Wolfe years after the war. We were in San Francisco, on one of those cable cars, and I happened to look out toward the sidewalk. There was Wolfe walking along like he didn't have a care in the world. I just sat up and stared. We got off at the next stop and I ran toward where he had been. But he was gone. I never saw or heard from him again, but I'd swear on the Bible that he was the guy I saw on the street that day."

Now that Svoray had the story of the missing dozen, meshing with what Pierron had said, Svoray was determined to find a means to use it.

There was one more thing. Nyer had received an invitation to go to France to receive a citation from the French government for the service he'd done for the French Army during the war when he and Tommy DeLion had been attached to it as scouts. He was considering it. It would depend on whether his wife would let him make the trip. She was opposed to letting him travel because of his health, but he hoped she might relent.

Svoray prayed that she would. If she did, then he was sure he would be able to persuade Nyer once in France to return to the hill, certain that, once there, they would find the diamonds in ten minutes. Svoray asked Nyer to keep in touch and let him know if and when he was flying to France. Svoray booked rooms for him at a hotel in Alsace, and arranged for a doctor to be on call just in case he was needed.

It was all in vain. Nyer's wife didn't care about the diamonds. She thought, as he did, that they were cursed and would bring only bad luck. She was concerned only with his well-being, and was convinced that a man with a heart condition should never make a long trip away from home. She refused to let him make the flight, and he received the citation by mail.

22

Playing the Media Card

So Svoray's hope that Nyer would lead him to the diamonds in person evaporated. But he had no time then to think much about it. A friend from his days in the Israeli Army called and asked for a meeting in Manhattan. He was working for a major international investigation agency on the theft of more than $400 million from a consortium of European banks by a one-time diplomat from Paraguay. The diplomat had vanished with the money, and Svoray's friend and his men had been unable to locate him. They decided to enlist Svoray's help, based on some of the police and intelligence work he had done in the past. And he offered to pay handsomely. Svoray accepted with alacrity, figuring the money would help pay off some of his debts and get him back to Alsace.

It took three trips to South America to track down the thieving diplomat and turn the information over to his friend's superiors, who then brought the man to justice. In the process, Svoray learned things that would ease his path in the years to come. The first, and perhaps the most important, was that in a media-saturated and -dominated world, journalists had nearly carte blanche to go where they wanted and act imperiously toward even the highest officials. The more important the journalist, the more prestigious his newspaper or magazine, or, especially, his television network, the more easily doors opened, the more officials were easily cowed. A midsize Israeli newspaper might work with low-level officials but not necessarily with higher-level bureaucrats. So Svoray upgraded himself to a correspondent for a major American network. A friend at the network helped: he would not provide credentials, but at least if anyone called to check, he would say that Svoray was working on a story in which the network was interested. That was enough.

And Svoray learned how to use money to grease palms and open doors. With the financial backing of his friend's investigative agency, he bribed doormen, cab drivers, contacts of all kinds, not without some resentment, knowing that the dollars he was handing over to a lowlife would have paid the rent at home, would have put food on the table, and would have bought his children new shoes. But it was necessary, and it worked.

When the case was finally resolved, and the former diplomat sent to prison, some money came his way, about $20,000. Hardly what he had been promised and certainly not the huge bonus he was led to believe he would receive if successful, but at least enough to keep his head above water. And enough to begin to look ahead once more to finding the diamonds.

He had his cover story now, the tale of the missing American soldiers, and he had figured out how to put it to use. He would be a filmmaker. He would spread the word that he was about to create a documentary on the missing dozen. He would invent a story to make his presence in the forests of Alsace—searching, digging—believable. The missing dozen, he would tell everyone, had left diaries of their war years—their reasons for leaving and their plans for the future—had placed them in a box, which, on that freezing night just before they departed, they had buried somewhere in the forest. This would now be Svoray's stated goal—to find that box with the diaries, film the search, and, once he had the diaries, make a documentary detailing the fate of the missing dozen. It seemed foolproof.

He was going to play the media card for all it was worth. No more fighting, arguing with the French. No more belligerence. No more stiff neck. He was going to be a good fellow, friendly and cooperative, working with proper authorization and the blessing of local officials.

He invented a couple of organizations, one in Washington, called the World War II Historical Society, and the other in Brooklyn, called New York Documentary Productions Associates, wrote some letters on their letterheads giving him an imprimatur, had them translated into French, and sent them off to the mayor of Sarreguemines and to the chief archivist in Strasbourg. (Though he did not know it at the time, did not know it until years later, Sam Nyer's hill and his forest did not fall within Sarreguemines' jurisdiction, and were not adjacent to the Saar; they were actually within the purview of the small towns along the Blies River, and so Svoray would have been better served had he buttered up to the officials of those villages.)

The first letter, from the World War II Historical Society, read:

Dear Mr. Svoray:

Following our meeting on 7-7-89, we are pleased to learn that you intend to return to France for the continuation of your search regarding the fate of the twelve missing soldiers.

Needless to say we attach great importance to your work in trying to solve one of the unsolved mysteries of W.W. II.

Since our last meeting it has come to our attention that one of the so-called "Missing Dozen" was probably seen in 1969 in Zurich. It is obvious that this does not qualify as concrete or even slight evidence. Yet it does make things very interesting. If in your research you should find those missing diaries, they will no doubt prove to be of very great historical value.

We thank you in advance for your valuable contribution in maintaining the memories of W.W. II veterans. As you may have realized we are almost with no funds to spare. Yet, if (and when) you discover the documents this will be a reward unto itself.

If there is any information, maps, documents, names, etc. that we can still provide, don't hesitate to call.

Yours truly,
Capt. (Ret.) N. Rollings

The second letter, from New York Documentary Productions Associates, read:

Dear Mr. Svoray:

This is to confirm our final arrangements concerning the preproduction work on the 64th Division's so-called "Missing Dozen."

While I must admit to a certain reluctance on our part to invest in this venture, we have now decided to come to the party by making the necessary funds available. The matter of participating staff members, legal fees, and arrangements regarding film rights, etc., will be discussed in a detailed letter from one of our lawyers, Gerthman, Salzman & Salzman.

May I add, in a personal note, that I am sorry not to be able to take part personally in your unique and exciting venture. If it comes off, it will no doubt be one for the books.

Good luck, Yaron.

Yours,
Andrew T. Stevens
Director

Using the word "film" was like uttering "Open sesame." Back came replies from France. It was wonderful that a movie was going to be made right where they lived. What could they do to assist the filmmaker? Just ask and they would provide authorizations, personnel if needed—anything he wanted. And when was he planning to arrive in Alsace to begin work?

That was the problem. Not for the first time, and not for the last, Svoray was out of money. He could see no way to finance a trip to France, let alone the sizable expense of organizing a dig. He was beginning to see himself caught in a trap from which there was no escape, burrowing deeper and deeper into a hole with no way out. It was like *Catch-22*. If he abandoned the search, there was no hope of ever finding the diamonds, no hope of ever rescuing himself from debt. It would have been an investment of years and money thrown away. But if he continued, he would be investing more time and more money with the distinct possibility of no end in sight. It was a conundrum. He argued with himself for a moment and realized there was just no way he was going to give it up. He knew without a doubt that somewhere among all those hundreds of foxholes, in all those stretches of dense forests—perhaps a thousand square miles— on one of the nine hills, was the right foxhole. In that foxhole was the pit with the diamonds. He would just have to keep at it until he found the one, no matter what the cost in time and money.

23

From the Air

While giving a lecture in Boston, Svoray met Steven Levin, a professor of modern history at one of the area colleges. As he did with so many people he met, Svoray told Levin the story of Sam Nyer and the buried diamonds, and the difficulties in finding them, in even locating the right hill.

"Have you thought about taking aerial photographs of the region?" Levin said. "That way, you'd have a clear view of everything, which ought to help pinpoint the location."

His suggestion struck a chord. Ori Svoray had come up with the same idea years before, but Yaron Svoray had dismissed it at that time. Now he decided to pursue it. As soon as he could, he would get back to Alsace, rent a plane, photograph everything, and then carry enlargements back to Nyer, sure that old soldier would take one good look and point out for sure which was his hill and which was the right side.

All he needed to do was raise the money. He was earning about $1,000 a month from the articles in *Hadashot,* more from the lectures and other jobs—barely enough to scrape by without any additional expenses. Mikhal Svoray bought into this new idea. They cut down on every expense considered nonessential, like books, presents, movies—everything. And they took on another job—folding and delivering Israeli newspapers and magazines across all of New York's five boroughs. They saved and saved, and eventually had just enough.

So it was back to France once more in 1990, this time by himself. From Charles de Gaulle Airport, he raced north and east toward Sarreguemines, feeling almost as though the car were driving itself, he was so filled with impatience and anticipation. He didn't bother to stop in the city and announce his presence or intentions; he drove directly to the forest and parked in deep cover. Le Grande was nowhere to be seen; if he had shown up, Svoray was convinced he would have run him down.

Walking out of the car into the forest, he was filled with visions of raging battle, seeing himself somehow as a surrogate for Sam Nyer on the day when he first trod this ground. He carried a large roll of light blue ribbon; he would tie it high on a tree in the middle of the forest, where it could be spotted from the air. But Svoray was no longer the young and agile soldier he had once been; now he was middle-aged and overweight. As he tried to climb to the top of one of the tallest trees in the forest, pulling himself up by the thickest limbs, he ripped the sleeves of a new shirt. Finally reaching the top, he tied the ribbon to a branch and let it flow out.

On the way down, he gouged his shoulder so badly it started bleeding profusely. He ignored it, a sense of satisfaction flowing through him as he stared up and saw the floating ribbon billowing out at the highest point. It ought to be very visible from the sky.

He headed back toward the car through the thick leaves that coated the forest floor, stepping through them without care or thought. And then, as his foot stepped into a pile of leaves, he heard a metallic click. He froze. He knew what he had stepped on. In 1975, as an Israeli paratrooper, he had gone through an extensive course on demolition, which, being very nonmechanical, he had hated with a passion. But his choice then was either that or commando training, and since demolition was three weeks shorter, at the end of which there was a two-week leave, he had decided to become a demolition expert. From the first day, he was constantly terrified. He learned about land mines, learned the sound when a land mine is stepped on, learned that while nothing happens as long as you stay frozen on the mine, once you step off, you've had it. The mine explodes and you lose a leg or a life. Don't panic, his instructors had said. Don't shift your weight, wait until your buddies appear, and, through complicated maneuvers, replace yourself with weights so you can escape.

But there were no buddies here. He was alone. He had been stupid, not paying any attention to his movements, and now he was frozen on a land mine. His stomach knotted. Sweat poured out. He didn't want to believe that half a century after all the battles had been fought and peace had returned, he had stepped on a mine. If he moved he was going to die, or at least lose some part of himself. He had to pee; his fingers fumbled, finally gripped and unzipped his pants, and he peed. He had to think clearly now, consider what he was going to do. He told himself there was no way he was standing on a land mine, no way it could be active after all these years, no way he was going to die. But he knew this was nonsense. He *was* on a mine, it *was* active, and he *was* either going to die or become a cripple. Self-pity flooded through him. For once he prayed that Le Grande would show up and come to his rescue. The forest ranger didn't.

There was only one thing to do. Leap off the mine and hope for the best. Lifting his foot, he threw himself as far away as he could, landing face first on the ground, tensing for the sound of the explosion.

Nothing happened. No sound. Nothing. He crawled away unsteadily and waited. Still nothing. His shoulder had begun bleeding again. He had to find out if he had really stepped on a mine, if there was really something there that had scared him half to death. He crawled back to the spot and dug. There it was, a round metal disk covered with mud, the center depressed inward—a land mine for sure. But it hadn't gone off. What miracle had prevented it? Under some leaves he found an old empty bottle of wine. He filled it with dirt, moved behind a tree, and threw the bottle at the mine. It hit the center of the mine on the first try. Nothing happened. He waited, then slowly and carefully moved closer. The mine was covered with rust, peeling off like cornflakes when touched. He picked it up and threw it to the ground as hard as he could. It broke in two. Unlike today's plastic mines, which last forever and never lose their deadly threat, metal mines from the past corrode over the years. The explosive charge inside congeals, turning into so much powdery muck. As a result, the mine loses any power to explode, to maim or kill. That was the case with this ancient mine. Svoray reached down and picked up the trigger mechanism and placed it in his pocket as a souvenir. To this day, it sits on his desk at home, a constant reminder.

He walked out of the forest to his car, ready to collapse from the tension and the fear. He drove not to Sarreguemines this time, but instead, across the border into Germany, to Saarbrücken, where he found a cheap hotel by the railroad station (learning later that it had once been a brothel), fell across the bed, and slept for twenty-four hours.

When he woke up, it was with the certainty that nothing was going to defeat him now, not the diamonds, not pain, not enemies, not anything—not after what he had just gone through. He was going to find those diamonds, and when he did all his worries would be over.

For the next two days he roamed through the towns on both

the French and German sides of the Blies, looking for an aircraft that would serve his purposes, a slow-moving aircraft that
could hover over the hills and allow him the time and the leisure
to take the photographs he needed. He found what he wanted at
a small airfield on the French side of the border. With hand ges-
tures and body language—flapping his arms like wings and
pantomiming taking pictures—and using pidgin English mixed
with the few French words he had picked up, he finally made
himself understood, and came to terms with a bubble-chopper
pilot named Jean. If Svoray returned in an hour, he would be
ready.

For an hour he wandered around the town, and when he
returned to the airfield there the pilot was, garbed now in a
button-down shirt and tie, leather flight jacket, old-fashioned
flyer's helmet, and aviator glasses. It was a contrast with Svoray's
old sweater, jeans, wool cap, and running shoes. They walked
over to the bubble chopper that looked more like a grasshopper
than something that would fly. It was unsettling, but since Svoray was on about as tight a budget as possible, he didn't think to
argue. It would have to do, and Svoray just hoped the man was
a good and careful pilot who wasn't about to act like some
World War I flying ace.

Jean motioned for Svoray to climb aboard. The cockpit was
small, cramped, and, with his bulk weighing it down, it leaned
dangerously to one side. Svoray braced himself against the
framework on the open side as the chopper rose into the air
with an ear-shattering clamor and tilted. He clutched tightly,
sure that at any moment he would be dumped out into the sky
to do a free-fall with unfortunate consequences when he hit the
ground. The chopper groaned, sputtered, and finally reached a
cruising altitude.

Now they could see for miles. On the ground, it was a clear, warm, spring day. In the sky, it was freezing. Svoray shivered uncontrollably as the frigid wind tore through the open cockpit.

Tapping Jean on the shoulder, he gestured toward the ground, trying to explain where he wanted to go, pointing toward the French-German border, toward the hills and forests. The pilot smiled and shook his head. He had his own agenda. Svoray kept pointing and shouting, trying to make himself heard and understood over the deafening roar, and the pilot kept smiling and shaking his head. Svoray could see all his plans crumbling. He was on a sightseeing flight, but not sightseeing what he wanted to see. In desperation, he pulled several bills out of his pocket and thrust them at the pilot. He looked at the money, then at Svoray, who pointed toward the border again and shouted, "There!" He grinned, took the money, and wheeled the chopper toward the border so suddenly that Svoray's lunch rose into his throat.

Within minutes, they were hovering over the border. Svoray pulled out his camera, a .35-millimeter Olympus, aimed carefully and steadily, and began snapping pictures of the ground below. He photographed the hills and the forests, found the blue ribbon dancing in the air far below, focused on it, and shot several pictures.

Suddenly, the bubble chopper dipped and turned with such force that Svoray had to clutch the door frame to avoid tumbling out.

"What are you doing?" he shouted. "Keep the damn thing still!"

But the pilot's expression said not only that he hadn't heard or understood a word, but that something else had caught his attention. He was staring up at something above the chopper that cast a huge shadow. Along with the shadow came a rumbling, a humming that drowned out the noise their machine was making. Suddenly, another chopper moved alongside, making theirs look like a speck of dust. It was a Cobra, and on the side was the insignia of the German Army. The Cobra moved back over them, forcing them down, forcing them to land.

As they descended, the pilot began yelling. Svoray didn't understand the words, but he got the drift. Since he thought Svoray was an American, he also thought they would get off easy. Little did he know. Here Svoray was, a Jew, an Israeli, son of survivors of the Holocaust, being forced down onto German soil by the German Army.

They touched down. The Cobra banked and landed. The pilot slashed his finger across his neck, telling Jean to cut the engine. Svoray knew that's what he meant, but the gesture had a darker meaning for him.

Jean turned off the engine and they sat and waited. Troops in German Army uniforms approached from somewhere and ordered them out of the chopper. They got out. They tried to offer explanations. A German officer held up his hand, ordering them to be quiet, and demanded IDs. With reluctance, Jean handed over his pilot's license, and his face said he was sure he'd never see it again. Svoray didn't think, didn't pause, just pulled out and handed over the fake letters of introduction he had written about the film on the missing dozen.

The German officer strolled away with the papers, while several soldiers kept watch over them. Suddenly Svoray realized that they must have been flying over some military exercise and the Germans thought they were photographing it for a nefarious purpose. They must have thought they were spies. That was just what Svoray needed, to be arrested in Germany for espionage.

Minutes later, the officer returned, shaking his head over the fake papers. He didn't say anything. He turned Svoray around with one swift move, holding him by the belt, and danced him awkwardly toward a large square tent. Looking around, Svoray oriented himself and realized they were about five miles from what he was certain was Sam Nyer's hill. They had flown into Germany just over the Saar. Now he saw a number of smaller tents in the woods, soldiers standing around them staring in amazement.

Svoray began to shake, frightened and angry, thinking that this wasn't happening, that this couldn't be real. Seeing Germans in uniform glaring at him, he began to visualize himself as the embodiment of all the Jews of half a century earlier and these soldiers not as the new Germans but as the old ones who had sent his people to extermination. He spit on the ground in front of one young soldier's boots.

An older soldier appeared. He spoke English. He didn't seem either worried or amused. He held the papers out to Svoray and said in American English, "So, what's the deal?"

Svoray decided to go on the attack. "I'm an Israeli journalist, on assignment for Israeli and New York media, and I'm doing a story on a battle fought here during World War II," he said. "I was so busy taking pictures of the battle site I never noticed your military exercise." And then he reached into his shirt pocket and pulled out his Israeli passport.

The officer reeled back as though struck across the face. He must have seen his military career going down the toilet, sent down by headlines proclaiming that the German Army had arrested an Israeli journalist.

After that, he spent about three minutes interrogating Svoray about the reason for his presence in the air over the area, and then, sure that he had done his duty, he ordered the younger officer to send Jean and Svoray back the way they had come. They moved back toward the helicopter and waited for permission to take off. Nobody made a move. Everybody waited.

About an hour later, a French police van arrived. The gendarmes spoke to the German officer. They pointed and began to laugh, then made some phone calls, got back into the van, and drove back across the border. They never approached Svoray and the pilot, and never spoke to them.

Finally, the young officer handed back Svoray's camera and told them to get into the chopper and leave.

So Svoray had the photos, and when he developed them they were good and clear shots of the area—the hills, the woods, everything. He left Alsace the next day and headed for New York, traveled almost immediately to see Sam Nyer and show him the aerial shots. He was sure that now Nyer would mark his exact location and the diamonds would be as good as in Svoray's hands.

Nyer looked at the photographs, looked at the maps Svoray had brought along, and tossed them aside. "Yaron," he said, "I was never in the air over this area. I have no idea why you think looking at these pictures and these maps is going to help. I never looked at a map, I never studied the area. I simply got there at night and stayed in the forest for two or three weeks."

Through his shock, he could hardly comprehend Nyer's words. But enough of his meaning seeped through for Svoray to realize that his efforts had been in vain. A waste of time and money.

24

Raising Money

Back home, Svoray began planning for his next trip. In half a dozen or more journeys to the region, he had found nothing. One day, he kept trying to convince himself, he would find the stones and then it would all turn out right. He was close to finishing his degree, and he and his wife decided it was almost time to return home to Israel. They had had enough of living in near-poverty in Queens.

But where was the money to come from for the family to go home and for him to go back to Alsace? One afternoon in Queens, playing volleyball, he met an oil-rigger named Barry Talbot from somewhere in the Louisiana bayous. After the game, they sat down to rest and chat. Talbot made a comment about Svoray's girth, wondering how someone that size could move with such agility.

"I wasn't always this fat," Svoray said. "But even so, I manage to keep myself in fairly decent shape." Then, in a lull, Svoray mentioned that he was in search of a treasure, but was out of money and wondering how he could finance another expedition.

It's like an oil exploration, Talbot said. One guy comes up with maps, charts, and geological studies and sits down with potential investors. He explains that this particular spot is where the drilling should take place, and if they put up the money, they could become rich. If they're lucky, there's an oil strike and everyone, including the guy with the charts who didn't put up a dime, gets rich. If they don't find oil, then the investors are the only ones who lose, and once that happens they're out of the picture, they have no further claim, even if someday, later on, oil is found as a result of other money put up by other investors. "What you're up to," Talbot said, "is right along that line."

Svoray liked the idea and began to put it to work. Traveling around the country giving lectures, he sought out people who might be willing to put up money on the long shot that it would pay off with the diamonds, and if it didn't, then all they'd lose would be their money, which they could well afford. In Los Angeles, Boston, half a dozen other cities, he sat down with potential investors, told them about the diamonds, and asked if they might be interested in backing the next dig. Nobody asked where the diamonds had come from originally, who might have owned them, who might have a claim on them. All they were interested in were forty rough, uncut diamonds and how they might be turned into cash, legally or otherwise. Svoray said he would recruit a team of experts (not saying experts in what, though the implication was there) who could take the diamonds out of France in a hurry, transport them to diamond centers where they could be sold, no questions asked.

The money came in dribs and drabs. When he had what seemed like enough (not enough to recruit a team or lay the groundwork for the sale if the diamonds were recovered, but enough for another trip to the site), he was ready to get on a plane and fly to France once more to resume the hunt. And then Svoray received a stroke of good fortune. In the summer of 1991, an uncle, who lived in England, sent Svoray tickets to fly over and meet him. Svoray jumped at the chance. He would head for Alsace first, survey the land for a few days, and then hop across the channel to England.

It was close to midnight when he checked into the hotel in Sarreguemines. Svoray stowed his luggage in the room and then decided to go to the hill in the dark, as Nyer and DeLion had done so many years before. He put a tape Nyer had made detailing his trek from the city to the hill into his Walkman. Then he began walking through the empty streets of Sarreguemines, ignoring the ways he had traveled in the past, this time following precisely the route Nyer and DeLion had taken when they had gotten off the truck and started marching.

As he walked, he tried to imagine what it must have been like half a century before. In his mind, this was not the modern, growing city of 1991, but a ruined place with homes pockmarked by bulletholes, fields littered with mines, German troops poised somewhere out there. Nyer had lived through a time of danger, of real peril, one of many young kids whose backpacks were loaded with ammunition, carrying fifty pounds of extra weight, kids half starved, kids who must have been terrified.

Svoray walked on, slightly out of breath on the uphill climbs. Nyer estimated that the march had taken two to three hours. Svoray walked for two hours, figuring that he could cut some time because he wasn't carrying the weight the troops had carried and he didn't have to tread as carefully through live mine fields. With Nyer's voice droning in his ears, after two hours he found himself at the same hill as before. He was tired and thirsty, and angry that he hadn't bothered to bring water with him. The damn bugs were eating him alive, a full moon and a billion flickering stars were in the sky, and he sat at the edge of the forest staring out at a startling and magnificent view. Spread out in front of him was the hill, sloping down to the river and to the village on the far bank. Exhausted, he made his way into the forest, found a foxhole, and collapsed into it, falling asleep almost immediately.

At dawn, he woke with a start. What am I doing, he thought? What else can I do to find the stones? The image of Uri Geller, a parapsychologist living in Israel who now made his living advising oil companies where and when to drill, raced into his mind. If he was so good at that, then maybe Svoray ought to seek out his help in the search for the diamonds. (Later, Svoray did contact him and they spoke at length. But after their conversation, Svoray decided that enlisting his help was not the way to go.)

Tired, parched with thirst, stiff from an uncomfortable night in the foxhole, Svoray trudged the miles back to the hotel, slept a little, and felt refreshed. In the afternoon, as he stepped into the lobby, the hotel manager accosted him. Svoray had been seen on the hill during the night, he said, and people were wondering why he would go tramping around the hills and forests in the dark. Svoray muttered something inconsequential and wandered away. Was he being paranoid, he wondered? Sarreguemines was not some little town in the boondocks where everybody knew everybody's business. It was the region's major city, growing rapidly, spreading out to encompass the nearby suburbs. Tourists arrived and departed constantly. Svoray did not think he was so extraordinary that he could not blend in. So why were people watching him, and what people? It upset him more than he wanted to admit. He needed help.

The person who might help was Marcel Pierron. So Svoray went out to his house, renewed the friendship, and then told him that he had returned to prepare for the shooting of a film on the missing American soldiers. Pierron was interested in the project, and his interest grew when Svoray showed him the various fake letters of intent. Svoray talked about making a big-budget movie when he had finally gathered enough background and had solved the mystery of the disappearance.

What could he do to help? Pierron asked.

Perhaps, Svoray said, he could speed things along with the local authorities, obtaining permission for Svoray to wander unobstructed, and not be constantly watched and followed through the forests and hills. Pierron promised to do what he could. Svoray would be away for several days, he said, and when he returned he would be back in touch with Pierron.

Svoray traveled to London to visit his uncle, a conservative, careful man who had been an early investor in the hunt for the diamonds. There he met Sara Ridgway, a beautiful woman with dark hair, high cheekbones, and green eyes, a former model and then a would-be writer who was a close friend of his uncle's wife.

During the evening, after dinner, Svoray again told the story of his search for buried Nazi treasure in the hills and forests of Alsace. Sara was fascinated, and began to talk about turning the story into a novel.

The next day they met again, and this time Svoray's uncle brought along a one-time Australian commando now living in England named Wesley. Wes, he said, with his muscles and his skills, could well be of considerable help in the search.

And so, with Wesley and Sara as companions, Svoray headed back to Alsace at the end of the weekend. Jonathan Bucksbaum, on his annual summer trip through France, joined them. They went right to Pierron, who handed Svoray an official letter stamped with the city seal of Sarreguemines giving him permission to dig unimpeded on the hill.

The first thing the next morning they rented a tractor, shopping in several towns in Germany until they found a midsize Bobcat with tanklike treads and a large forklift and a digging arm. It was similar to one Svoray had used during his early days on a kibbutz. He considered himself probably the worst tractor driver who ever lived, a real klutz behind the wheel. With the tractor in tow, they headed for the hill, beginning to dig in what seemed to be likely foxholes. In the distance, Forest Ranger Le Grande watched with sharp, disapproving eyes. They were not very adept at the excavation and, after several hours of fruitless digging, they headed away, leaving the Bobcat behind in preparation for another round the next day.

When they returned to the hill in the morning, the tractor refused to start. During the night, someone had poured sugar into the fuel tank. Svoray was enraged. Wesley and Bucksbaum tried to calm him down, and they and Sara drove back to the rental agency, leaving Svoray alone on the hill with the maimed Bobcat to wait for their return.

He seethed. Then matters got worse when Le Grande and a deputy Svoray was convinced was smirking at him appeared. Svoray lost his temper and raced toward them, looking for a fight. All he could think of was that this old guy was out to do him in, to stop him from finding the diamonds. If it wasn't for him, they'd be in Svoray's hands already. He wasn't thinking about their uniforms and official positions or shotguns or anything else—he simply wanted to punch the smirk off the deputy's face, to smack Le Grande right through his beard. His momentum sent him smashing into Le Grande, who stumbled backward. Svoray started cursing him. The deputy came between them and tried to shove Svoray away. Instinctively, Svoray head-butted him, and even as his forehead smashed into the deputy's mouth, Svoray knew he had gone too far. He was blaming them for the sugar in the tractor, and he wanted revenge. (Later he learned that they weren't the ones responsible; it had been a local farmer who didn't like it that the Bobcat had been driven through his field, and he was out to teach them a lesson, to show that he deserved respect.)

The only thing that saved Svoray from jail was the sudden appearance of Wesley and the tractor mechanic. Wesley grabbed Svoray's shoulder and tried to pull him away, telling him to back off and apologize to Le Grande and the deputy. Svoray knew he was right, that if he didn't the whole treasure hunt would probably come to a sudden and unpleasant end, never to be revived. But he was so enraged, he couldn't bring myself to say anything.

Then Marcel Pierron, Bucksbaum, and Sara came to the rescue. They were suddenly there, and Pierron convinced Svoray to move away. They gathered around Le Grande and his deputy, whose lip was swollen and bleeding. They talked to them, calming everyone down. Le Grande showed restraint. Maybe he was used to people exploding, what with all the smugglers and poachers he had to accost every year.

When the air had cleared, the mechanic repaired the Bobcat, at considerable expense, and then the digging began again, under the watchful eyes of Le Grande, who stared from a distance. They sifted through the upturned earth and found nothing. For another two days, the tractor turned the soil and the leaves in the foxholes, and still they found nothing.

And a dark cloud was gathering. Pierron was becoming a little frigid. He reminded Svoray that while he would soon be leaving, Pierron lived in the area and Svoray's outbursts were doing him no good with his neighbors. Depression crept in. Svoray began to think everyone was ganging up on him. He was digging in every hole he could find, and unearthing little more than dirt. Was he in the wrong place, on the wrong hill, in the wrong forest? He couldn't believe it. He believed the diamonds were buried there. He believed his triangulations spanning all

Nyer's landmarks were correct. And yet the diamonds eluded him. He had uncovered many pieces of old soldiers' clothing, shoes, spent bullets, but nothing else. What was he doing wrong?

The party decided to call it quits. Another foray ending in failure. They spent a final afternoon and evening with Pierron, had another wonderful dinner, Svoray trying to make amends as best he could, and then began packing to return home, dreading to tell his wife that, once again, nothing had come of the journey.

Just before leaving, he decided to take one last look at the area to convince himself that he had the right hill, the right forest. They drove across the Blies, and suddenly, looking back toward the hill, he began to wonder if perhaps all this time he had been on the wrong side of the hill and the ridge, concentrating on the side that looked back toward Sarreguemines. Yet the defense lines the French had constructed in 1914 and again in 1939 looked not south and west toward Sarreguemines and the Saar, but the other way, north and east, toward the Blies and Germany and all the towns that bordered that river. He speculated that one of the hills overlooking the Blies and those towns was the right one. He had no choice at this point but to return home, but he decided that when he came back again, he would begin looking at other hills in other forests. Surely there would be hills facing north and east from which the landmarks could be seen and triangulated, and surely there would be other foxholes. He was certain that the right one was still out there, waiting.

25

Neo-Nazis

But the return would have to wait. When he landed in New York, there was a message from an old friend who was working for the FBI. Could they meet without delay? Svoray's wife was not happy at the prospect. Why would he go running off on some new adventure when he still had all his studies to complete? And what about his lectures and the assorted odd jobs that would earn the money they needed now, and the money they would need if they were to go home to Israel?

While her reasoning made sense to him, he still could not resist the temptation, the smell of action. So he went to Brooklyn and learned that his friend was now part of a joint FBI–New York Police–Alcohol, Tobacco and Firearms task force investigating the illegal sale of guns and silencers to Brooklyn Russian-Jewish mobsters by Israeli gangsters. The task force was looking for someone who could infiltrate a buy-and-bust sting. Only another Israeli could do the job, since only another Israeli would be trusted by both groups, and only another Israeli would understand the special street dialect they used. Svoray was the guy they wanted.

He wanted to do it, but feared his wife's reaction to his playing cops and robbers one more time, not as a paid cop but as a volunteer. Three of the top brass in the task force showed up at their house and, after considerable pressure, she ultimately relented. Svoray made the contacts in an Israeli nightclub, set up the sting, and then starred in the videotape (which he has never seen) as the task force appeared and made the busts. Though it had been an exhilarating and successful adventure, taking a couple of months, he not only never received any thanks from the task force, but never even earned a penny for putting himself in danger.

Then it was back to studies, back to lectures, back to odd jobs here and there, back to the growing sense that soon, very soon, they would be going home to Israel, where, at least, they had friends and family. Yet the diamonds kept drawing him, and he kept trying to put them on a back burner. They wouldn't remain there. They kept gnawing at him, demanding that he unearth them and claim his fortune.

If he was not back to square one, he was close to it. But he was not about to give up. He had already invested too much time and too much money, and he was determined to keep up the search until he had those diamonds in his hands. The dream of the treasure obsessed him: he considered the gems his, and he finally boarded a plane once more in 1992 and headed for France.

Back in Alsace, he took stock. He was sure now that he had been exploring the wrong side of the hill. From then on, he would concentrate on the other side, the one facing Germany across the Blies rather than the Saar. But, still, was he really sure this was the right hill? He went over all Nyer's accounts. The troops had marched out of Sarreguemines for two to three hours until they reached the hill and the forest. Perhaps he had underestimated a little. Perhaps they had marched for a little longer, but certainly not much longer. If so, then perhaps three or four other hills also fell within the purview, not just Kopfberg, the hill that Svoray had always thought was the right one.

He went across the Blies, stood on the river by the town of Blies Schmeyen, and peered up at the hills. There was the one he knew, had marked. But moving along the Blies toward the other towns, toward Blies Guersville, Bliesmengen, Bliesbolchen, Frauenberg, and more, he could make out other hills that Sam Nyer might have reached and where he might have been dug in—Knopfwald, Spir, Auf der Helle, others. He began to explore them, finding foxholes, as well as mementos of battles. More troubling, from every hill, he was able to see all the landmarks Nyer had studied and memorized. If not Kopfberg, then which was the right one? He plowed his way through them all, triangulating, marking likely foxholes, digging in some and finding nothing, planning which he would excavate next. He was certain that Kopfberg was the right hill, that somewhere in its forests was Nyer's foxhole, but he could not risk ignoring the possibility that he was wrong, that it was another hill altogether.

Late one afternoon, tired and mud-covered from his latest foray, he returned to the hotel in Sarreguemines. As he entered, the hotel manager approached. Like so many others, he now knew of the supposed plans to make a documentary on the missing American dozen and of the hunt for the buried diaries. And he knew of the repeated failures to find them.

Perhaps, he said, it might be of assistance if Svoray talked to a German soldier who had fought against the Americans during the battles in the area in 1945. He knew of someone who had done just that and might be willing to share his memories. The man's name was Gerhard Schultz. Svoray ought to meet with him.

Svoray had nothing to lose, and, perhaps, a lot to gain. If this Schultz had, indeed, served with the Wehrmacht against the Americans on the eve of the invasion of Germany, then perhaps he knew of the bombardment of the tiger tank, and knew of the German return-shelling of American forces that had wounded

Nyer, knew then where those forces had been. If he did, then it was possible he could finally spot Nyer's position, Nyer's hill, and Nyer's forest. It was worth making the detour, taking the chance.

So Svoray got into his rented car, crossed the Blies, and drove along the autobahn to Frankfurt. From the hotel manager he had received two names, Charlie Muller, who was something of a military historian, and Gerhard Schultz. It was a start.

From his room at the Inter-Continental Hotel, he called Muller's number, introduced himself as Ron, a journalist and filmmaker interested in arcane aspects of World War II. He had been told that Muller knew a man named Gerhard Schultz who had served in the Wehrmacht on the Alsatian front, and Svoray was especially interested in the battles fought on that line. Could Muller put them in touch? Muller was intrigued, not about the interest in Schultz but about "Ron's" background in filmmaking. He, too, he said, was a filmmaker, and he would help Svoray find Schultz. As a matter of fact, he said, Schultz lived not in Frankfurt but in German Alsace. Meanwhile, as a fellow filmmaker, would Svoray be interested in attending a group he helped sponsor and seeing a film he had been instrumental in making?

Svoray agreed. Anything to make the right contacts.

But he was totally unprepared for what awaited him in the Frankfurt basement where the film group gathered for its screenings. Draped on the wall was a large Nazi flag, twisted cross and all. The group members were men, many dressed in Nazi-like uniforms with armbands sporting what was nearly a duplicate of the swastika. And then the film began. Svoray had to hold tight to avoid vomiting. It was pornography, but worse. A pornographic snuff film, a group of masked men raping a child of perhaps ten and then slitting her throat and gloating as she died, the screen filling with blood. It was a moment that would haunt him for years and would later lead him into another investigation that occupied a good portion of the mid-1990s.

But at the time he attempted to stay focused on gathering clues about the diamonds. That was the sole reason he was in Frankfurt. The next day, Charlie Muller introduced him to Schultz, who had traveled from his Alsatian home for the meeting. Not only had he been a member of the Wehrmacht, but he had also belonged to the SS. He had served on the front in Alsace—though what he knew about the events of February 1945 was useless—but he had also been a guard at the notorious Buchenwald concentration camp. There was something else. Somehow he had managed to retain his *Soldbuch,* the full record of his service to the Third Reich. For a price, he might be willing to sell it.

Having just seen a gathering of neo-Nazis at a snuff film, having read about the resurgence of the neo-Nazis and skinheads in the press almost daily, and now having met a real live Nazi from the old—and the worst—days, Svoray felt he could not just let it pass. He would have to do what he could to expose this menace. So he contacted the Simon Wiesenthal Center in Los Angeles with the news of Schultz's *Soldbuch* and what it contained, and shortly thereafter flew to the West Coast to meet with the center's leaders who had been working for years to unmask the new German right wing. They asked if Svoray would agree to attempt to infiltrate the movement and document what he discovered.

The infiltration lasted ten months in 1992–93. Before it was over, he had moved from dealing with the lowest levels, the skinheads, to the highest, those supposedly respectable Germans who were working to restore the legacy of Hitler behind cloaks of probity. He gained their confidence and become privy to their secrets. Facing constant danger if his cover were blown, given the violent nature of these people, Svoray compiled lengthy dossiers on the leaders of the neo-Nazi movement not merely in Germany but in Argentina, South America, Australia, and the United States. The results: hearings before the U.S. House of Representatives Foreign Relations Subcommittee on Human Rights soon after his work was over, at which he testified at length, and then a debriefing by the German Ministry of the Interior and the German Federal Police to spell out the inner workings of the neo-Nazis worldwide. This led to a toughening of Germany's anti-Nazi laws and raids on party headquarters.

It was something, but far from enough. Nobody was ever arrested. Nothing happened to any of the leaders. If the neo-Nazi movement was crippled, it was crippled only for a moment, then revived with perhaps even more vigor. And it made Svoray a marked man in the eyes of the neo-Nazis.

While this penetration of the movement did little to directly advance Svoray's quest for the diamonds, it did lead him deeper into the age when the world had been enmeshed in war and the slaughter of innocents, the time when the diamonds had been plundered by the Nazis and then liberated and carried to the Alsatian foxhole by Sam Nyer and Tommy DeLion. And Svoray's actions in Germany did end up creating opportunities that would eventually advance the search. But from then on, he was inundated with threats and hate mail, forced to have a bodyguard whenever he crossed the border into Germany. That bodyguard, Ako Hintzen, was head of one of the most important security firms in Germany. From the moment Svoray and Hintzen met, a bond formed between them, and Hintzen became one of Svoray's closest friends. He also came to play a major role in all that followed in the ongoing hunt for the diamonds.*

The Svorays moved back to Israel in 1992—just before Svoray's infiltration of the neo-Nazi movement—rented a house, and began to live like human beings for perhaps the first time, not worrying for the moment about the looming presence of the wolf at the door. Once more, Svoray began to plan another journey to Alsace, another search for what he considered *his* diamonds. On four separate occasions during that journey into the subterranean world of neo-Nazism, he had detoured to Alsace, roamed the hills for a day or two, dug in this foxhole or that one, and found nothing. He was still not going to give up.

But much as he planned and thought about the next venture, he could not rid himself of the nightmare scene in that Frankfurt basement, the screening of the snuff film, the rape and slaughter of that young girl. He dreamed about it, and woke up in a cold sweat. Every time he looked at his young daughter, the images kept returning, haunting him. He knew with a suddenness and clarity of purpose that everything else would have to be put aside. He would have to do something about the snuff-film business or he would not be able to live with himself.

As a detective with Yamar, he had gained considerable knowledge and insight into the workings of the seamiest parts of the underworld, and he had made scores of contacts in that world. Some of them owed him favors. It was time to call in some of those IOUs.

He had no idea that, in doing so, he was setting out on a

---

*For the full story of the infiltration and exposure of the neo-Nazi movement, see *In Hitler's Shadow* by Yaron Svoray and Nick Taylor, Doubleday, 1994.

worldwide journey that would take him from Tel Aviv to Bangkok, from New York to Belgrade, and far beyond—a journey that would plunge him into the depths of degradation, the world of the pornographic snuff-film industry, where death is purveyed as a form of recreation—and that this journey would fill the next two years of his life, from 1994 to 1996. Nor did he realize how little impact the investigation would have on anyone but himself. If he managed to expose some of the purveyors, if he managed to open up what can only be described as a bottomless pit of filth, when it was over, the smut peddlers who specialized in snuff went about their business with hardly a pause.*

---

*For the complete story, see *Gods of Death* by Yaron Svoray with Thomas Hughes, Simon and Schuster, 1997.

26

A Hunting Expedition

All during the time Svoray was engaged in this terrible search into the snuff-film business, the diamonds were never far from his mind. Whenever he was in Europe, he made weekend side trips to Alsace. There he invariably spent time with Marcel Pierron (though Svoray was certain Pierron never really believed the story that he was planning a documentary about the missing dozen and was sure he was after something else—he didn't know what, but he never asked—and they maintained an abiding friendship), cemented relations with the officials of Sarreguemines (spreading gifts around and helping to restore the town hall and other public buildings), and continued to spend a day or two trekking through the hills and forests, digging into long-forgotten and -abandoned foxholes. As always, he never found anything but old relics of the two wars, and there were even moments when he wondered if, perhaps, he might actually have found Nyer's foxhole and dug in the wrong part of it, missing the hole where he and Tommy had planted the gems.

And then Svoray was seemingly diverted again. Only later did he come to understand that this diversion was actually bringing him around full circle, leading ever closer to the diamonds. Though he didn't realize it then, this diversion was a link to the past, to the Holocaust, the pivot around which everything in his life was revolving.

He was in a gelato parlor in Milan near the end of his efforts to fight the snuff peddlers, making contacts that might open other avenues into that vile trade. The contacts this day were two mercenaries who, among other sordid dealings, organized for a very high price hunting parties for the bored and wealthy. They videotaped these hunting expeditions so the hunters would have mementos of their exploits. The thing was, however, they were not hunting animals, but people. It was the rumor of the videotapes that had led Svoray to them. He thought that guys who videotaped killings of one kind might be a link to videotaping of another kind—snuff, for instance.

As they were discussing arrangements for a forthcoming expedition to which Svoray was invited, two young girls of about thirteen walked into the parlor, trying, without much success, to look and act like little sexpots. They sashayed up to the counter, ordered gelatos, and began licking them with gusto. One of the girls handed the proprietor an American hundred-dollar bill. He stared at it, glared at them, shook his head, and ranted angrily that there was no way on earth he could change an American hundred. The girls looked as though they were about to flood the place with tears. Svoray decided to come to their rescue. He got up from the table, walked over to them, and offered to change the bill into lire. They looked relieved and delighted. The girl handed him the note and he peeled off lire in exchange. They smiled, thanked him profusely, paid the proprietor, and then rushed out, licking their cones. Svoray watched as they reached the street, where they immediately threw the gelatos into the gutter and raced away.

His two companions were laughing.

"What's so funny?" Svoray asked.

"You've been had, mate. Those two little hookers just screwed you out of a hundred."

Svoray looked at the bill. It looked, felt, and smelled real. "How?"

"That shit is counterfeit. It may look good, but it's pure shit. Those girls work for people from Central Europe who come here with bags of phony American. They take the bills, wander around town looking for suckers willing to exchange them for lire or francs or pounds or whatever. Which you did."

Svoray shrugged. He was out a hundred, but at least he had a souvenir, and maybe he'd had another learning experience. He folded the bill carefully, put it in his wallet, and didn't think much about it then.

On a Friday, a week later, he was along for the ride on one of the hunting parties. It was not without mixed feelings, wondering whether this was just another of those side trips that was leading him ever farther from his goal, and wondering, too, if this wasn't some fantasy, men out hunting other men. They were sitting in the second-story windows of a shattered building on the edge of the war-ravaged town of Vukovar in Croatia close to the Hungarian-Serbian border. The two middle-aged hunters were dressed in *Soldier of Fortune* mail-order garb and carried expensive, customized rifles with the latest in telescopic sights. They had each paid $15,000 for whatever hunting pleasure the organizers could devise.

In the distance, there was sudden movement at the edge of the next village. One of the hunters peered through his sight, aimed, and began firing. He reloaded and fired, kept reloading and firing. About six hundred yards to the east, Svoray saw someone who looked like an old man fall to the ground. The video camera whirred, preserving it all so that he would have a record of his successful kill, if, indeed, he'd actually hit anyone.

Then the other man started sighting and firing. Despite the telescopic sight, the only thing he ever hit after firing off dozens of rounds was a grazing sheep in a nearby meadow.

Svoray felt stupid and uneasy, and even a little sick to his stomach. This certainly wasn't what he had expected, and it certainly did not look as though it were going to lead anywhere into snuff, or anywhere else that mattered to him. He figured he would desert this expedition as soon as he could safely do so.

Then, suddenly, some armed men appeared on the other side of the meadow and started shooting in their direction. The two intrepid hunters seemed to have no taste for battle against people who fired back. They turned tail and raced back to the Mercedes parked outside the building, screaming that they had to get out of there fast. The guy who had videotaped their kill handed them their mementos and then the car—with Svoray and the two hunters inside—sped away.

About two miles outside Vukovar, they were stopped by a roadblock. It hadn't been there earlier when they had driven through. The irregulars manning the roadblock took one look at the rifles the hunters were carrying and decided they wanted them. For the next few minutes, there was a tug-of-war over those rifles, and it began to look like more serious trouble was about to erupt. Svoray decided to stop it before it did. He pulled a rifle away from one of the hunters and handed it to the irregular soldier, who grinned with satisfaction. The hunters and their escorts dashed back to the Mercedes and took off, leaving Svoray stranded in the middle of a war zone.

Perhaps because he had helped the young soldier get his desired rifle, perhaps because he had been abandoned in a strange land, he was invited back to the soldiers' camp to have tea with them. While they were talking and sipping their tea, they began to hear shouts and screams from a bombed-out building nearby. A woman was about to be gang-raped by three men. Svoray and a couple of the soldiers went to her rescue, managing to extricate her from her peril and turn the would-be rapists over to those in charge of the camp.

Immediately afterward, mortar rounds started to fall in the area. The shelling ceased almost as soon as it started, but apparently it was the prelude to an all-out attack. Before the fighting intensified, the woman who had just been saved from the gang-rape (her name was Sophia) rushed from the house to a battered Russian-built Lada. Svoray had no desire to get caught in the battle, so he raced after the Lada, climbed in beside Sophia, and they headed away from Vukovar toward Sarajevo.

Once they reached the city, Sophia steered him to what had once been a townhouse. It was her port of exit from the war, she said. The house was now home to thirty-nine refugees also seeking escape from the war. All but two were women and children. Svoray was introduced to a man in his early seventies named Alexander Muskovitch, who either owned the house or was in de facto possession of it. Taking Svoray by the arm, he led him into what had once been a kitchen but now seemed to be a laboratory, a room filled with microscopes, magnifying glasses, and paintbrushes, the walls adorned with paintings that looked very familiar, beautiful copies of masterpieces that filled the world's museums, such perfect replicas that only an art expert could have spotted them for what they were. Staring at them, taking in the other items, Svoray understood immediately just what this Muskovitch did. He was a forger, and an expert at his work.

One of the things he was doing then was forging identity cards and other papers for those who desperately needed them if they were to escape to freedom. Sophia appeared in the room and began arguing with Muskovitch about the price of the papers he was preparing for her. She didn't have enough money and she had no way of getting what she needed, yet she was desperate to flee. Svoray had rescued her once; he decided to do it a second time, especially because she was the reason he wasn't at that moment caught in the middle of a firefight in Vukovar.

"How much does she need?" he asked Muskovitch.

"Two-hundred-fifty American, for everything," he said.

Svoray sighed, took out his wallet, counted the money, and handed it to him. As he was doing that, his fingers touched the hundred dollar bill from Milan. Lifting it from the wallet, he handed it to Muskovitch and, knowing now for certain just what it was, he asked, "What do you make of this?"

Muskovitch took it, held it, then put it aside without saying anything, and went back to preparing the papers for Sophia. But every once in a while his eyes moved to the bill. He would stare at it for a moment, then return to his work. It took him about two hours to finish. He handed the well-made forgeries to Sophia, and he and Svoray both followed her out of the house and watched as she got into the Lada and drove away.

They returned to the house, to the laboratory. Now Muskovitch picked up the hundred-dollar bill and studied it closely, seemingly captivated by it. He took a magnifying glass and pored over it. He looked up. "Not many people could do that," he said. "Very few. Where did you get it?"

"Some girls had it in Milan. They needed change and I changed it into lire for them."

"Did you know what it was?"

"Not at the time."

Muskovitch smiled and said, "You help that woman and she's not even your girlfriend. I tell you, you're a *mensch*. You know what a *mensch* is? In Yiddish, it means a man, a real man." He studied Svoray. "You are no gangster. Gangsters I know. Those who did this—" and he rolled up his sleeve and revealed faded blue numbers tattooed on his forearm, "they were gangsters. So, who and what are you?"

Svoray did not answer immediately. Muskovitch was a Jew, a survivor, but who knew what else in this land, Yugoslavia, which the Nazis had occupied and where those who collaborated are still honored by many.

Muskovitch sighed. He turned and went to a cabinet, opened it, removed two candles and a yarmulke, a bottle of red wine, and two goblets. He poured the wine, put the yarmulke on his head, lit the candles, and intoned the ancient Hebrew Sabbath blessing over the candles. As he began the recitation, Svoray rose, put his hand over his head, and joined him.

"Ah," Muskovitch said when the prayer ended, "so you are a Jew. I knew it."

"And an Israeli, a kibbutznik," Svoray said. "And my name is Yaron Svoray."

That evening they came to know and understand each other well. Later, Muskovitch took the hundred-dollar bill again and studied it under a bright light, moved it this way and that, folded it, creased it, crumpled it, mashed it, grew excited. He carried it to a microscope and examined it under the magnification. He took his time, and then looked up. "My friend," he said at last, "this is magnificent, a masterpiece."

"So, it's not real."

"It is the best counterfeit I have ever seen. Perfect, except for three tiny, really minor flaws caused by the paper, not the chromium plates or the ink or the press. These flaws only someone like me could detect."

"So, who makes them?"

"I wouldn't know. I hear rumors, but I am not in the rumor business. I deal in facts, what I know. And I know this is not some *farkochta* operation out of a small-time garage. Not with this paper, with this ink, with this kind of attention to detail.

This is intaglio offset printing. This kind of work can only be done by a government. It takes time, training, resources. Only once before in my life have I seen this kind of work."

"When?" Svoray asked.

"I will tell you. It is not a short story. It goes back fifty years, to a terrible place called Sachsenhausen."

27

KZ Sachsenhausen: The Master Forger

There was a man named Solomon Smolianov, a Russian Jew, an outcast because he was a criminal. A master forger, he was a man who moved from place to place all over Europe turning the real into the fake, mastering the art of making pounds, francs, rubles, deutschmarks, zloty, currency of all kinds. When the Nazis overran Europe, suddenly Smolianov's artistry was in great demand: He became a man everyone wanted to know, everyone wanted as a friend, for he was a man who could save lives with a favor—with a passport, an identity card, or a travel document indistinguishable from the real thing.

Smolianov's reputation spread beyond the Jewish community, and came to the attention of the Nazi overlords. In 1938, he was arrested and imprisoned in Dachau. He was there for only twenty days, purchasing his release with forged documents and forged money he made for ranking officials in the camp.

Free again, he continued his old line of work on the outside. Once more, the Nazis searched for him, finally found him in the summer of 1940, and sent him to Mauthausen concentration camp. He survived there, too, by forging scrip for the guards, who protected him. In 1942, he was suddenly told his days at Mauthausen were over. But his next destination was not

Auschwitz or another of the death camps. The Nazis had a use for him, a very special use. He was sent to KZ Sachsenhausen.

Located twenty-five miles north of Berlin, *Konzentrationslager* Sachsenhausen, near the city of Oranienburg, under the jurisdiction of the SS, opened it gates to its first inmates, mainly political prisoners, in the late summer of 1938. By the beginning of World War II, there were nearly twelve thousand prisoners, most of them communists, social democrats, labor leaders, and Jews. By the spring of 1940, inmates were dying by the hundreds every week as a typhus epidemic raced through the camp and the SS refused to provide any medical care and not even the minimum food rations necessary to support life. So the first crematoriums were built. After Germany's invasion of the Soviet Union in June 1941, the population of Sachsenhausen increased dramatically with a flood of Soviet prisoners, more Jews, and other "undesirables." In the winter of 1943, new installations were constructed, specifically designed for the extermination of prisoners. To show off the efficiency of this installation, the SS invited high-ranking Nazi officials to witness the slaughter of ninety-six Jews. A month later, gas chambers, rather than bullets, became the preferred method of mass killing.

It was at Sachsenhausen that Solomon Smolianov met the young Alex Muskovitch, who became his protégé. They were not marked for manual labor or for death, but for something else, something very special.

They were housed in a secret barracks with 144 other Jews, all with exceptional talents as chemists, mathematicians, painters, printers, engravers, bankers, craftsmen, and photographers. They had been gathered from slave-labor camps all over occupied Europe. For two years, the Nazis had been using them to create perfectly forged British five-pound notes. The aim, according to what the prisoners learned, was to manufacture millions and millions of such forged notes and then have the Luftwaffe drop them all over the British Isles, flooding the country with fake currency. The Nazis believed that this would not merely disrupt the British economy but might even bring about its collapse.

If these prisoners could perfect such forgeries, they were promised the best food, the best medical care, warm blankets, heated barracks, even tobacco. If they could perfect these forgeries, their lives would be spared; if they failed, they would die along with the rest of the Jews of Europe. But among all these experts, there was not a master forger, and no matter how they tried, they could not do what the Nazis ordered.

Until Solomon Smolianov arrived. He examined the efforts that had been made, and dismissed them. Much was of value, he said, but one thing would inevitably lead to failure no matter how expert the work. The paper being used was Turkish linen, which was wrong, so any notes printed on it would be discovered quickly. Smolianov had the answer to the paper puzzle: British notes, he said, were printed on paper made using water from the Hull River mixed to precise formulas with old mail bags.

Under Smolianov's direction, the paper formula was matched, and the production of forgeries began in earnest in the fall of 1943. By November, about 200 million five- and fifty-pound British notes had rolled off the presses. But by then, the Luftwaffe had lost control of the skies and there was simply no way to drop the notes over Britain.

A new scheme was devised by SS leader Heinrich Himmler himself. He ordered the director of the Sachsenhausen forgery project, Bernhard Kruger, to set his Jews to work forging American hundred-dollar bills. Once more, the effort seemed doomed to failure. No matter how hard they tried, the experts in the secret section were unable to produce acceptable forgeries. Until, once more, Solomon Smolianov stepped in. He developed a retouching process that made the forgeries nearly indistinguishable from the real bills, so the printing presses began to churn out hundred-dollar bills.

But it was too late. The Allies were closing in, and the war was about to be lost. Before the liberation of Sachsenhausen on April 22, 1945, the bulk of those forged American hundreds and British five- and fifty-pound notes were gathered and transported to a secret hideout in the Austrian Alps, along with gold, diamonds, and other valuables. Some would be used by the fallen Nazi leaders who managed to survive and elude capture; they would provide the means for them to begin new lives under assumed names in Latin America, the Middle East, and elsewhere. They would be able to pay their protectors and live well. Some, too, along with the printing presses used to manufacture the counterfeits, would be hidden in sealed, waterproof boxes, together with plans for the Fourth Reich, and sunk deep into the waters of Lake Toplitz in the Austrian Alps, waiting for the day when the Nazi movement would be reborn.

When the Allied armies overran Sachsenhausen, the forgery unit was gone. About a week earlier, the forgers had been gathered and transported to another secret and now long-forgotten camp named Radl-Zipf, a satellite of the dreaded KZ Mauthausen. There they were supposed to labor on. But not for long. On May 5, the Allies arrived, liberated Radl-Zipf, and so saved the lives of those secret Jewish counterfeiters. Every one of them survived. Many found new lives in the West, in Canada and the United States. Others went to Palestine. And some, who traveled east in search of their families, were taken to the Soviet Union and put to work for the KGB, or to East Germany, where they found employment in the Stasi. With the collapse of the Soviet empire in 1991, some sold their expertise to the highest bidders.

As for Solomon Smolianov, he disappeared with Radl-Zipf's liberation. A few years later, he surfaced in Brazil, the proprietor of a flourishing children's bookstore. Until his death in 1975, he regularly sent out notices to his best customers that he had come upon a rare and very valuable first edition of a children's classic and was offering it to the highest bidder. He had, as well, he informed them, come upon a number of very rare, intricately designed, handmade children's toys.

28

Escape

Svoray listened to Muskovitch's story about Smolianov and the Sachsenhausen counterfeiters with amazement. In the middle of war-torn Bosnia he had come upon a man who had been part of yet another of the top-secret Nazi schemes that used Jews to advance their aims, just as they had used the Jews at KZ Vught and the diamonds that had been sent there.

"What I'm telling you," Alex Muskovitch said when he ended the story about Solomon Smolianov, holding out the counterfeit hundred, "is that only a government can organize an operation of this magnitude. Do you think that just anybody can buy currency paper, special-formula inks, printing presses for money, even if they know what to do with them? Then there is the artwork and the engraving presses. To produce bills like this, you have to set up your own De la Rue or Tombrook, those major money producers of the world. You have to get your paper from companies like Porotel's, the ink from SICPA in Switzerland or SICMA in Belgium, the presses from Giorgi in Switzerland; and those companies are monitored very closely. And then there is the expertise and some way to get the Americans to look the other way.

"But someone is doing exactly that."

"Who?" Svoray asked.

"I already told you," he said, "I don't deal in rumors."

In the morning, Muskovitch kept looking at his watch and seemed impatient to have Svoray leave. When he saw the expression on Svoray's face, he said, "I'm sorry to be such a bad host, but I'm working very hard to get the people out of here. It is not easy and not in the usual way." He motioned to the forgery tools strewn around the kitchen. "But it is urgent that they leave as soon as possible, and I, too, must go."

Svoray understood that. It was bad enough to be trapped in a war zone. It was worse for children. It was worse, still, for a Jew in a country where Jews were still viewed with antipathy.

Muskovitch looked at Svoray. "And you? You are staying?"

"For the moment," Svoray said. "There are some things I have to do."

Svoray spent the next week ferreting around the underworld in this war-torn land, looking for clues about the counterfeits. The result: Before he knew it, he was a hunted man.

It was time to get out, and get out fast, if he were to stay in one piece. The way to escape was to find Alex Muskovitch again. As his search began, Sophia turned up again, and together they made their way to the forger's home, praying that he himself hadn't already left by then. They reached his house, knocked on the door, and, after a wait, the door opened. Alex Muskovitch was surprised to see them. He was also very worried. The house was teeming with people. Svoray told him that Sophia and he had to get out of the country fast and needed his help.

He switched from English to Yiddish and said, "Do you remember what I told you about getting the children out of Yugoslavia? Do you remember Moses?"

Then Svoray understood. Alex Muskovitch had made arrangements and someone was coming to take the desperate out of Sarajevo.

"When?" Svoray asked.

"Soon. In twenty-eight hours. And you, what will you do?"

"We'll try to hide," Svoray said, "and we'll contact you tomorrow."

"Be careful," he said.

They were. Twenty-six-and-a-half hours later, they were back at Muskovitch's door. This time he greeted them warmly and led them through back alleys and the houses of his friends to reach the loading area for the buses that would take the children to safety. The loading area was chaotic, parents hugging and kissing their children goodbye, wondering if they would ever meet again.

Near one of the buses, Svoray saw a member of an international Jewish agency, someone he had never met. Svoray tried to tell him of his predicament, but he had no time for that. He and several others were busy loading the people—children, women, old people, about a third Jews, the rest of other religions and ethnicities, all caught in this vicious war—onto the three buses and doing other essential things. Svoray wondered how much money must have crossed palms to permit these buses to leave, this convoy to cross borders.

The men in charge of this rescue mission had clipboards with the list of passengers. As each one boarded, the name was checked off. Sophia's name was not on the list, of course. Muskovitch interceded. He gave up his own seat for her. She leaned out the window to say goodbye, and, without thinking, Svoray gave her another counterfeit hundred he had come into possession of, since he knew she had no money. In an emergency, who would know?

Then the buses departed. Muskovitch and Svoray were alone.

"I want to thank you for what you did for my friend," Svoray said.

"We do what we must do," he said. "You're going to be okay?"

"Now that I'm on my own, I think so. And you?"

"We are never on our own," he said.

"You'll find a way out?"

He nodded. "And you?"

"If there's a way, I'll find it."

He smiled, turned, and vanished into the darkness.

Svoray found a way, hiding in the back of a truck heading for Romania, and the next day he was home in Israel.

29

Zuckerman

Not long after his experiences in Croatia, Svoray was in Holland giving one of his lectures, this one dealing not merely with terrorism but also with his descent into the world of snuff. After the lecture, he was introduced to a man named Levi who was particularly fascinated by the subject, since he owned several of Amsterdam's leading brothels and churned out a vast amount of pornography on his printing presses. They talked for a while and then he said, "Listen, I know a man who lives in the suburbs, a weird old guy. I'm sure he knows a lot of about what you were talking about, pornography and snuff films. Would you like to meet him? He's one of the leaders of the homosexual community."

That Friday evening, Levi took Svoray to the synagogue and introduced him to a small, wiry, little man in his seventies. Levi told him about the lecture and said he thought this man and Svoray ought to get together to explore the subject further. The old man bridled. He said he knew nothing about such things. And further, the subject of snuff was nothing compared to what he had seen in the camps. Svoray apologized for Levi's presumption and they chatted. Svoray said he would be interested in hearing more about what had happened in the camps, especially since he had infiltrated the neo-Nazis and collaborated on a book about the neo-Nazi movement. As it happened, the old man had read the book. He gave Svoray his phone number and suggested that they talk.

Svoray called and was invited to the old man's home, about half an hour from Amsterdam. He opened the door but, instead of inviting Svoray in, he suggested that they go to a coffee shop a few blocks away. In all the times Svoray visited him after that, he was never invited inside; they always went to that coffee shop to talk.

The old man talked about himself, about the camps in which he had been imprisoned, about the things he had been forced to do. As he talked, Svoray had a sudden revelation. This man was a direct link to Sam Nyer and the pouch with its diamonds, the first he had ever chanced upon. He could hardly contain himself as he listened. From him, Svoray was sure he would learn the origin of that pouch, would discover the journeys it had taken. This night he was back in the hunt.

For the old man had been at KZ Vught, where he had been the chief appraiser of diamonds and other gems and valuables. But he incurred the wrath of one of the prison guards by refusing to turn over a particularly valuable stone to him, one that had been earmarked for a higher-ranking guard. So in early September 1944, he suddenly and without any warning was put on the list of those to be transported to one of the death camps in the East; in his case, the first stop would be Westerbork. He did not know it then, did not know it until much later, but within a week of his departure, many of the other prisoners at Vught would be sent on their way as well, to Sachsenhausen and Ravensbrück, and farther east.

His stay at Westerbork was brief. And then he was on his way east again. On the train, he learned that being a homosexual meant death when they reached their destination. "One of the men on the train told me that the Kapo where we were going was a Jew, and if a Jew on the train was able to work, he was spared and sent to labor for the Third Reich. Homosexuals went immediately to the gas chambers. He said, 'You'd better find a way to trade that pink triangle for a Star of David.'

"I asked, 'How can I do that?'

"He said, 'You'd better find a way or you'll be ashes.' "

He found the way. In the cramped boxcar, men died by the dozens. He went to one of the dead, took his Star of David and his identity, and when the train reached the death camp and the roll call was read, he was Lieb Zuckerman, a Jew, and he was selected for the slave-labor detail.

About a month later, he was shipped off again, this time to KZ Sachsenhausen, where he was assigned to the *Diamond-kommando*. This was the unit of Jews ordered to gather diamonds and other valuables that could be used by the Nazis to buy safety when the war was over.

"Five barracks away," he said, "in Barracks 18 and 19, there were other Jews doing something very secret. We never knew just what it was they were doing, but we knew it was important because they were protected." What they were doing, of course, was turning out counterfeit pounds and dollars under the expert direction of Solomon Smolianov.

The war was nearing its end, the Russians closing in. "I knew I would survive," he said, "and I knew what I had to do. I killed my first Nazi the day the camp was liberated. From then on, I was out for revenge. I would stand by the side of the road, near an American Jeep, and when the crowds of displaced Germans shuffled past, I would point out the Nazis I recognized hiding among them and then I would kill them. There were American Jews in the Army and they looked the other way, and sometimes they would give me names and I, together with others who felt as I did and who joined me, would track them down. If they were Nazis, they always had loot with them. When I left the camp, all I had were my striped pajamas. Six months later, I was a rich man, I had a fortune that I took back with me to Holland, and, once home, I was no longer this Lieb Zuckerman. I took again the name of my father."

Back in Holland, he went into business, dealing in antiquities and artifacts, in gems, in a dozen different things. He made fortunes. But remembering the camps, remembering what had happened in them, he gave part of his income every year to charities benefiting the survivors.

30

A Changed Mission

Now, at last, Svoray began to realize that for a full decade his life had been one long search. Yet he had not really understood what he had been searching for, nor why. His investigations had begun with Sam Nyer's story of the buried Life Diamonds, and had led from KZ Vught to KZ Sachsenhausen and all those other places of hell on earth beyond the imaginings even of Hieronymus Bosch or Dante. He had learned about Lieb Zuckerman and Jacques Furth and Solomon Smolianov and all the others, especially the children, forced as slaves to labor unto death. He had focused on the Life Diamonds, acquired to save the Jews, and the counterfeit currency, created to save the Nazis. And he had come to know perhaps more than anyone should want to know about Hitler's Nazis, modern-day neo-Nazis, and all those other purveyors of unspeakable and barely imaginable horrors.

He decided to go to Yad Vashem, the Holocaust museum and memorial in Jerusalem, and talk with Professor Yehuda Bauer, the world-renowned Holocaust scholar. Svoray told him about Smolianov and the counterfeits created at Sachsenhausen and about the search for the buried rough, uncut diamonds, mentioning that Sam Nyer had seen the letter *K* on that purple leather pouch.

"That letter," Professor Bauer said, "that *K,* is undoubtedly the first letter of *Konzentrationslager* Vught, KZ Vught as it was known, the concentration camp in Holland, a very special place, with a very secret task. Not many people know about it anymore. It is what they call one of the "forgotten camps." But at that time, during the war, it was the clearinghouse for the most precious loot seized from the Jews."

When Svoray came away, he saw what he should have seen at the beginning, and what he had begun to sense increasingly during the search for the diamonds and the related, and seemingly unrelated, avenues down which he was led. He understood at last that the diamonds did not belong to him, nor even, if he were to find them, would they profit him. His dreams that the diamonds would pay off all his debts, would make him rich, would even afford him a life of luxury on some pleasure island, suddenly evaporated. He knew it would never happen. It was as if he finally realized that the diamonds were, indeed, cursed. The curse was a black cloud, or perhaps a red one filled with blood, that rained down disaster on anyone who thought of the stones as his, who sought them for his own enrichment.

And he knew, too, that at the center of everything—the diamonds, the counterfeit currencies, everywhere he had turned and traveled—was the Holocaust. It was the awful glue that bound everything together: No matter where he looked, the Holocaust cast its sinister shadow.

He knew then that he would continue to search for the diamonds, but from now on with a different purpose. He still hoped that he would find them, if not immediately then someday not too far in the future. This was something he had to do, bring closure to this long and, until now, frustrating and selfish search. When he told his wife, she was relieved and delighted. From the beginning she had known that the diamonds did not belong to them and that if Svoray found them, they were not his to keep. From the beginning, she had watched his obsession with dismay.

The task now was twofold: to develop a realistic plan for finding the diamonds as well as a plan for what to do with them once found. To accomplish both, he would need help. In 1998, he traveled to Cologne and met with his friend, Ako Hintzen, the man who had acted as his bodyguard during the neo-Nazi troubles and was now as close to Svoray as anyone. They discussed how to return to the hill in Alsace. Svoray had visited the region only sporadically and only for an hour or two of fruitless searching in the past two years after spending so much time and energy there in the years before. Luckily, he had not caused problems recently—with the forest ranger, with the curious local citizens, with anyone. The answer, of course, was to hide in plain sight, and the way to do it was to press forward with the documentary on the missing American dozen, to announce that at last he was going to begin preproduction and move rapidly into shooting.

About six one morning, Ako woke Svoray and said it was important that he get dressed immediately to meet someone who might help him. They drove for half an hour through the dark streets of Cologne, arriving at an exclusive gym on the outskirts of the city. Hintzen went inside, emerging a few minutes later with a tall, athletic, blonde woman wearing shorts and a T-shirt, a towel draped around her neck.

"I want you to meet Barbel Schaefer," he said.

She smiled, shook Svoray's hand with a hard, muscular grip, and told him in perfect English that Hintzen had talked about him to her frequently. They sat in Hintzen's bulletproof Audi and chatted, mainly about Svoray's infiltration into the neo-Nazi movement, and Svoray discovered that she was a rising star of German television, on the verge of becoming, people said, the continent's Oprah Winfrey, her daily program on RTL Network shown all over Western Europe.

A few days later, they met again. This time Svoray told her about the diamonds, and about his continuing problems with

French bureaucrats despite their frequent commitments to put no obstacles in his way.

"If you want my help," she said, "I'm willing to do what I can."

So, he enlisted her help, and with her camera and technical crew, journeyed to Sarreguemines. Now he had the name of a real TV personality to impress the authorities, someone known and watched throughout the region. Her name and the sight of her camera crew were enough to make them very welcome. They were offered any help they needed, lent full cooperation by local officials. They could go where they wanted, film what they wanted, talk to whomever they wanted without any hindrance. They stayed on a couple of days, then left. A few days later Svoray returned, only now he was a respected and appreciated visitor, given carte blanche. Over the next several days, he photographed and filmed a comprehensive survey of the region, from rooftops, backyards, hilltops and forest edges, everywhere and everything, including all nine hills from every conceivable angle.

With that record, he and Barbel Schaefer flew to the United States, immediately went to see Sam Nyer, and spread out all the photographs before him. Nyer looked at Barbel and his eyes lit up. He took to her, seemed ready to do anything she asked, anything that would please her. What would please her, she said, was if he examined the photographs. He studied them carefully, going through each and every one, then stopped, pointed, and said, "That's it. That's the hill. That's where our foxhole was and that's where we buried the diamonds."

He had, of course, said the same thing more times than Svoray could count when maps and other photographs had been shown to him in the past.

But the way he said it to Barbel Schaefer, with such conviction, Svoray was sure there was no mistake now. This was the right hill. It was Kopfberg, the hill he had pinpointed from the beginning, the hill with twin forests separated by a large meadow with border markers running its length, one forest in France, the other in Germany.

Now it was time to find the stones at last. The question remained, of course, how to dispose of them once they were retrieved. Who would take them and use them to benefit the displaced, the survivors of the Holocaust? This was the only possible use for them, the only way to lift the curse that had hung over them, afflicting all who came in contact with them.

Svoray explored many avenues and most turned out to be dead ends.

Now that he understood that the diamonds were not his to keep, he sought ways to turn them to the benefit of those in need. He was naïve. He thought it would be a simple matter. If he finally found the diamonds, he would hand them over to the right organization and let it use them to benefit those in need. After all, who would stand in the way of someone wanting to do good? Little did he know. He was about to learn that, under law, it is almost impossible to make an unencumbered gift, no matter for what purpose.

He contacted his friends at the Simon Wiesenthal Center, at Yad Vashem, and at other major Jewish organizations. Would they be willing to take possession of the diamonds when and if he found them, and use them for the proper purposes?

The response stunned him. They would like to help, they all said, they would love to take the diamonds and do good with them. But it was impossible. To take them, he was told, would be asking for trouble, trouble that would embroil the recipient in legal entanglements for years to come. Where was the provenance? Who had owned them? Where had they come from? If found in France, the French government would demand that they be turned over to it, because under French law anything discovered in that country belonged to the state. Then there were the survivors. How many among them, and how many descendents of those who had perished in the death camps, would surface to claim that the stones rightfully belonged to them, to claim that the diamonds had originally been the property of one or more long-dead relative? No, Yaron, everyone said, good luck to you, but we can't take them and the trouble that will inevitably accompany them.

The curse, it seemed, was still in force. But perhaps there was a solution after all, a risky one; but where else was he to turn? He contacted the man who had been known in Sachsenhausen as Lieb Zuckerman, the man whom the Nazis had used at KZ Vught to appraise and sort the diamonds, and explained the dilemma. Zuckerman listened. If Svoray so desired, he said, he would take the diamonds and see that they went where they would be used for the purposes Svoray desired. There was one caveat, however. He might have to take some of the proceeds to cover his expenses.

Svoray agreed. Did he have a choice? When and if he found them, they would meet in Luxembourg and Svoray would pass them on to him, and hope for the best.

It was the moment to bring the eleven-year journey to an end. It would be done under the cover of the documentary on Sergeant Wolfe and the missing dozen. Svoray planned to hire an army of professional filmmakers to shoot the diversionary search for the diaries in one forest, a distance away from the real hill and forest, thus engaging the attention of local citizens. At the same time, he would bring a specially trained crew of excavation experts onto Kopfberg. With the most modern tools, they would pinpoint Sam Nyer's foxhole, dig, and exhume the diamonds.

One last time, in the spring of 1999, before his final foray, Svoray went to Alsace, to Kopfberg, entered the twin forests, roamed around them, and triangulated the foxholes using Nyer's landmarks. He found three foxholes in each of the forests that seemed most promising, foxholes from which all the landmarks could be seen. In one of them, Svoray was certain, the diamonds must be buried. He marked them and then departed to set the final scene in motion.

PART IV

End of the Journey

31

Into the Forest

Early in the evening of July 9, 1999, a few months after Svoray's last visit in the spring, an eight-member search party gathered for the first time on a hill overlooking the Blies River, a tributary of the Saar, on the meandering border between France and Germany in Alsace. The sky was overcast, threatening rain. For more than a decade, Yaron Svoray had been wandering the hills and forests of the region, over thousands of square miles, trying to spot the exact hill, the exact forest, the exact foxhole where, on a freezing February night in 1945, Sam Nyer and Tommy DeLion had buried the purple leather pouch with its forty rough, uncut diamonds.

This, he was sure, was the right hill; it matched in every detail the descriptions that Sam Nyer had given him. On this steep hill, named Kopfberg, there were twin forests, joined at the crest like an inverted U by more dense forests, the twins separated by a hundred yards of meadow and cultivated fields, border markers running the length of the clearing, one forest in France, the other in Germany. All the landmarks cited by Nyer were visible from the meadow and from both forests—the river below, the village of Blies Schmeyen (on which the first artillery shells had fallen in an engagement between French and German troops at the start of World War II) rising up from it on an opposite hill, and still higher on that hill the church steeple, the farmhouse and farmyard, the footbridge, and all the rest, and then beyond still more forest where, half a century before, German troops had been dug in. To the west, barely discernible, the Saar meandered. South of the hill, hidden by the forests, over the crest, lay the town of Sarreguemines, or Saargemund, as the Germans called it. If Yaron Svoray's calculations were correct, this was the right place, and it would be the culmination of his long and frustrating search for the buried diamonds.

Svoray had been planning for this day for years, convinced that success lay at the end. But if the diamonds were not found within the next forty-eight hours, then all his efforts would have been in vain. He had decided to give it this last effort and, if he failed, to finally abandon the search, tell the officials of the nearby towns the truth about his activities over the previous decade, and let them start their own treasure hunt. What the result would be he did not know, but he did know that he could no longer devote all his time and energy, all his life, to this mission. The diamonds were buried on this hill, that he knew, but perhaps he was not destined to find them. If so, he would depart the field and leave it to some other treasure hunter, or leave the diamonds to rest in peace forever. But not before he had done everything possible to retrieve them.

He had dreamed how this weekend would go. His dream was grandiose. It would be like a lavish Hollywood epic. There would be professional camera crews, sound and lighting experts, cinema technicians of all kinds, an army of extras recruited from the surrounding towns and cities—the whole extravaganza witnessed by invited guests, including the mayors of all the surrounding towns and other local officials. They would move off to another hill, another forest, and occupy themselves for the day, and even the next, filming the diversion, the tale of Sergeant Wolfe and the missing dozen. And while they were thus occupied, specially trained Israeli commandos with bulldozers, tractors, and earth-moving and excavating equipment would advance into the forests on Kopfberg and open up every foxhole until the diamonds were found.

It was not to be. Svoray could not afford this dream. He had simply run out of money once more, was far overdrawn on his bank, was maxed out on his credit cards, owed a dozen different people who had lent him money to pursue the search over more than a decade, and was able to borrow only enough more to barely meet his own expenses, if that.

Even his alternatives had come to nothing. In the spring, he had met and held a number of discussions with Jim Murphy of the CBS Evening News, who expressed interest when Svoray explained what he intended to do. Murphy expressed interest. If Svoray would agree, and if he found the diamonds, Murphy's show would send its own producer, correspondent, and camera crew within two hours of the discovery, film the diamonds, and have them—or at least one of them—appraised, and put the news on the air that night. The story would be a big one, he said, and would most surely be of major interest to one of the prestigious CBS shows like *60 Minutes*. Then perhaps one of those seventeen-minute segments on *60 Minutes* would reprise the adventure and its finale. People close to Svoray were dismayed at that prospect. If the story appeared on the CBS Evening News that night, it would certainly be on television shows around the world within hours. It would be something people would talk about over the office water cooler the next morning and then it would fade from public consciousness. Any later attempt by Yaron to tell the full story in a book or a film would seem like stale news. Besides, when the news leaked out, everyone who thought he had a claim to the diamonds—descendents of Holocaust survivors, the French government, others—would surface and demand the return of what they would assert was rightfully theirs. The courts would be filled with lawsuits for years to come. It was an appalling prospect. Svoray capitulated to the pressure from his friends and backed away from CBS.

Still, there was Barbel Schaefer. He felt he owed her a great deal. Soon after he met her and they became friends, she had provided help when he needed it, had opened doors in Sarreguemines, had enlisted the cooperation of the area's officials, and had allowed him to put together all the details in photographs and maps so that, when Barbel and he had shown them to Sam Nyer, the old soldier was able to say, "That's it. That's my hill."

So, a few days before the gathering on Kopfberg, Svoray met with her brother, Martin, the producer and main adviser on her show. The dig was imminent, Svoray said, and because of his promises and her interest, he was inviting Barbel and her cameras to go along and film the end of the hunt. He expected the enthusiasm she had displayed in the past to rise once more, and the eagerness to be in on the final moment to override every other consideration. But Martin Schaefer was stone-faced. "Barbel is burned out, exhausted. She needs a rest and she's on vacation in Ibiza," he said. "She won't be back. She won't be going along with you." Svoray understood that behind Martin Schaefer's blunt statement lay the simple fact that he, and perhaps she, had lost whatever faith they had in the treasure hunt and were not about to commit their time and money to a wild-goose chase.

Svoray was devastated. With Barbel and her camera crew recording his triumph, this final act would have been preserved for posterity, would be proof against all doubters. Now that, like so much else, was not to be. He kept the news to himself, initially telling only Ako Hintzen. He was worried that if he told others, they, too, like Barbel Schaefer, would back away. He was wrong about that, but he had no way of knowing it, for blow after blow had made him cautious, wary of doing anything that might upset the delicate balance. When Hintzen heard about Barbel Schaefer's withdrawal from the project, he was not displeased, despite Svoray's reaction. When Hintzen first met her and introduced her to Svoray, Barbel Schaefer was the rising television star in Western Europe, an Oprah Winfrey aiming to be the next Dan Rather. But pressure for ratings had made the show deteriorate, and, as far as Hintzen was concerned, she had become more exploiter than reporter. Her presence and imprimatur would, he felt, hurt rather than help the cause.

Still, it was obvious that, no matter what, a camera crew of sorts was necessary to film the diversion (as other cameras, still and video, were essential to record the actual digging and unearthing, if that were to be) and so keep the curious at a distance. Hintzen stepped into the breach. He booked Svoray a hotel room and paid for it, so Svoray would not look like a pauper or a beggar, then arranged with a local German television station to hire a four-person crew to do the work.

Hintzen did more. When Svoray's original grandiose plan collapsed, he had intended to hire day workers from the area to do the actual digging. Hintzen was furious at the idea and immediately vetoed it. He would provide the men to do both the digging and to maintain security. "You can't trust anyone, especially strangers, with the true story of what you'll be doing," he said. "You can trust my guys absolutely. They'll give their lives for me. They can dig and they can guard us. They know how to keep their mouths shut, and they'll do whatever else is needed." Svoray didn't argue.

And so, on this early July evening, under leaden skies, a small party of treasure hunters gathered on Kopfberg. The eight-man party, led by Svoray, was composed of four Jews—Rick Kaufman, a Canadian and one of Svoray's closest friends, two Americans, Mel Berger and Richard Hammer, and, of course, Svoray—and a four-man German security team led and recruited by Ako Hintzen, head of one of the most important security agencies in Germany.

Hintzen and his three Germans, tough guys all, security experts all, were in some ways interchangeable. They were all tall. They were all agile. They were all extremely fit. They were all self-assured, confident of themselves and their abilities to meet and overcome any emergency, any danger. They were all representative of the new postwar Germany, men determined to put the Nazi past to rest, to make sure it would never reemerge, to heal the wounds and scars it had left on the world. All were experts in the arts of self-defense and attack. And all were armed. Who knew what peril might suddenly appear should a vast treasure be found and an attempt be made to take it away?

Hintzen, about to turn forty, was the leader. More than the leader. He was second to Svoray this day, and sometimes his coequal. Nobody could have filled the post better. He was a German, born and bred. "Our roots go back to Wolfgang von Goethe," he says, "though my dad says there's nothing special in that, because Goethe fooled around like crazy." He considered himself the black sheep of his family, the one who had not followed his forebears into respectable professions. His mother's older brother, Dr. Erhard Bahn, was a writer and professor of philosophy at UCLA. Her younger brother spent years in Africa as a highly placed executive for Siemens, then moved back to Munich where he married an Englishwoman whose family included members of the British parliament. His father's sister married Dr. Paul LeSat, a law professor and member of the Federal Republic of Germany's government. His maternal grandfather was a high-ranking officer in the German Navy in both

World War I and II, and was badly wounded during the Second World War. His paternal grandfather was a prominent surgeon who served during the war in both France and Russia, while his grandmother was outspoken in her anti-Hitler opinions and was arrested several times, escaping serious punishment only because of her husband's position. His father, who was in the *Hitlerjugend* (Hitler youth) as a child, though he became a fervent anti-Nazi later, studied medicine after the war, specializing in hip and other joint replacements and becoming chief of his hospital. His mother, who met and married his father while both were students at Freiburg University, made a career as a physio-therapist. His brothers and sisters all carved out careers in these professions.

Ako Hintzen went his own way. His own way was to master the martial arts, found a security agency, Dynamic Protection Security, one of the most important in Germany, and spend his time and energy protecting important people like the Dalai Lama, analyzing major events like the assassination of Israeli Prime Minister Yitzhak Rabin, and working undercover to unmask terrorists and members of the German Nazi and neo-Nazi movement. "You'd think, looking at me, that those guys would have jumped at the chance to have me be part of their thing," he says. "I mean, if you're looking for someone who fits the old Nazi description of the true Aryan, I'm that. But they took one look at me and told me to get lost.

"I believe in the warrior myth," Hintzen says. "Warriors recognize each other and respect each other and they don't have to prove themselves to anybody. I work for honor and higher justice, hoping to help the world and to improve it, and I have an outstanding sense of justice. I believe in good, although I always have contact with the bad. I believe one must absorb what is useful and eliminate what is useless. If you do the right thing, nothing can harm you. One of the most important events in my life was meeting Yaron Svoray and working with him."

There was Eren Aydogan, a tough, handsome, muscular, and very self-assured twenty-seven-year-old of Turkish descent, second to Hintzen in his security agency. Eren's grandparents had been farmers in the Kurdish mountains, and his father, a cook. Eren's father moved to Germany in the 1960s, first working for Mercedes in Stuttgart, then settling in Langenfeld. In 1978, he sent for Eren and his sister. After primary school, Eren became a shoemaker and began studying tae kwon do and other aspects of the martial arts, earning a black belt. Within seven years, he was German and European champion in kickboxing. About this time, he joined Hintzen's Dynamic Protection Security agency and soon rose to a trusted position as second in command. Though he became a German citizen, he has faced and battled constant trouble with jingoistic Germans, who consider Turks something less than true Germans, who refuse to recognize them as citizens of their country.

There was the slightly older Chalid Amale, almost too handsome, born in Morocco of a prominent Muslim family. His maternal grandfather is a sharif in his Moroccan community, his paternal grandfather a high-ranking police official. His father was a Moroccan hotelkeeper who moved to Spain, where he continued in that line of work until he moved to Paris, again as a hotel executive, before returning to Morocco, where he married Chalid's mother. Then, in 1967, the couple moved to Germany where Chalid and his brother Omar were born. Though a German citizen, Chalid, like Eren, was not recognized as such by the neo-Nazis and other right-wingers because of his Moroccan background. And, like Eren, after graduating from high school as an electronics technician, he turned to the martial arts, perfecting skills in a number of areas, winning black belts in several. He had been with Hintzen in D.P.S. for eight years, working undercover in antiterrorist investigations, and as a protection specialist for many of the VIPs who have turned to Hintzen. "He's a nice and charming guy," Hintzen says. "All the girls love him, and he loves sweets. The only problem with him is that he sleeps too much."

And there was forty-eight-year-old Helmut Weirauch, born in Hamburg of a Polish Jewish father (who had been an officer in the Polish Army and, when Poland was conquered, a German prisoner of war) and a German Protestant mother. Their marriage was annulled soon after Helmut's birth, and he has not seen his father since. In school, in Saarland, to which his mother moved in 1956, he was constantly harassed by other German kids who called him *Judenbenge* and other derogatory names. After finishing school, he became a miner, held a dozen different jobs, until deciding to pursue a career in medicine. He took evening classes after work, passed the examination to become a medical assistant, then went to the University of Hamburg, where he studied intensive anesthesiology. He went to work in a hospital after graduation and, since 1990, has been chief of anesthesiology. In his spare time, he turned to sports—first boxing, becoming German junior champion, then soccer, and then karate, earning a third-degree black belt and becoming a member of the German national team. Not satisfied with all that, he took to running distances, and has run a number of marathons. Helmut and Hintzen met in 1979 in the south of France, where Helmut was teaching karate and windsurfing, and became close friends, Hintzen calling him "my elder brother." Most of his adult life has been spent in Saarland, where he married and had two children, a son, who is a student, and a daughter, who aspires to a career on the stage or in films—"but not Hollywood," she says, "in Paris or London or Berlin." When Hintzen asked for his help, Helmut has never failed to respond, so when Hintzen called on him to join the search, Helmut agreed without hesitation.

Then there were the Jews in addition to Svoray—Berger, Hammer, and Kaufman.

Mel Berger, in his late forties, was a modern, postwar, observant Jew, devout, a synagogue member active in his congregation, a celebrant of the Sabbath and all the holidays, able to blend his religious faith with a successful career in one of the most cutthroat of businesses, as a literary agent for the powerful William Morris Agency. Early in the spring, Alan Kannof, head of William Morris' New York office, and his wife, Ellen Umansky, a Jewish studies scholar on the faculty of Fairfield University in Connecticut, attended a lecture by Svoray at the college, sponsored by Umansky, during which the search for the diamonds was discussed. Kannof was fascinated. He invited Svoray to meet with him at his office, and there introduced him to Berger. Berger was equally captivated by the story of the forty Life Diamonds, and became determined to shepherd it into a book. He put Svoray together with Richard Hammer, one of his clients with a long-standing, deep, and abiding concern for history and the Holocaust—a man who had written more than twenty books and won several major awards. When Svoray told him about the plans for the dig, Berger was intent on being part of it. Nothing was going to stop him. He had never been to Germany before, nor to Paris, which lay both at the beginning and the end of this journey. But more important was being in on something with vast and altruistic implications.

Born a Jew, Richard Hammer, had always identified himself as a Jew and had said more than once that he would be a Jew as long as there was anti-Semitism, though he had long ago lost his faith and considered himself at best an agnostic. The idea of a personal, caring God vanished for him with the Holocaust and its aftermath, with the things he saw, experienced, and wrote about for *The New York Times* and in several books on the American South during the civil rights struggle and in Vietnam, and with the death of a young daughter. A lifelong commitment to the underdog, to those in peril and in need, had often undermined his objectivity as a journalist, had often colored the things he wrote, tipping the balance and, he sometimes felt, perhaps preventing him from being the reporter he should have been. About that, though, he had few regrets. The younger of his two sons had abandoned a promising future as an actor and political activist and turned to a new life in semi-isolation on the extreme fundamentalist fringes of ultraorthodox Judaism, rejecting, often with vituperation, his past, his old non-Jewish friends, even members of his family. While Hammer remained true to his roots, he wanted no part of such unquestioning acceptance of doctrinaire dicta.

Meeting Svoray and joining him in the search for the diamonds stolen from the victims of the Holocaust was not merely an adventure, but more—the possibility of doing something noble, and writing about it. And so, despite the many problems involved, he was determined that nothing would prevent him from being part of this moment. Even if the diamonds were not found, this would be something worth doing.

At thirty-five, Rick Kaufman was a hard-eyed man who exuded the sense that he would be a formidable ally to have and a dangerous enemy to oppose. He was a man with a golden touch. A mathematician of the highest order, he had graduated from McGill University with honors and then moved on to graduate school to pursue an advanced degree in mathematics. But other interests sidetracked him. He became something of a ski bum, good enough to make the Canadian Olympic team. He ran. He drove race cars. But above all, he discovered that he had a mind for business, for making money. His first foray was buying a small ski lodge, modernizing and glamorizing it, then selling it at a huge profit. He moved into electronics and communications, and made another fortune there. He built and developed shopping malls in Canada and the United States, began to buy property around lakes and mountains in remote areas, build resort cottages, and waited for the city dwellers to come to him. They came, in droves.

Kaufman and Svoray met on a Yom Kippur holiday in Svoray's hometown of Caesarea at the home of mutual friends. During the evening, pressed by his friends to give an update on his quest for the diamonds, Svoray told his story in detail, the first time he had ever done more than merely relate parts of it. Kaufman was fascinated and offered to help. Recalls Svoray, "There must have been a thousand people who said the same thing, only they either didn't mean it or they wanted something out of it. But Rick was different. He showed up at my home the next day and repeated the offer. He didn't want anything in return then. He just thought this was a fantastic story that ought to be told. He said, 'When you start to make money, then we'll see. But you're the worst guy with money I've ever known. So when you start to make it, let me handle it and make it grow.'"

When the final dig was impending, Kaufman initially had refused to attend. The diamonds, he said, echoing Sam Nyer, were cursed and he didn't want to come near them. But after the rejection by the Schaefers, Svoray called to tell him what had happened. Kaufman heard him out, and then said, "Don't worry. I'll be there. And I'll do a few other things."

These eight men, most strangers to each other, gathered on July 9, 1999, on a mud-covered lane at the edge of one of the forests on Kopfberg, that hill that was half in France, half in Germany.

This was the initial look that anyone, save Svoray, had of what they would face the next day when the dig for the treasure would begin. It was hard to believe that this pastoral setting, the rolling green meadows and fields merging with the darker green of the woods, dotted here and there with farms and cultivated fields, had been the terrain over which ferocious battles had been fought for five hundred years, that beneath the fertile soil lay the bones of long-forgotten soldiers, millions of pieces of metal, abandoned weapons, land mines, all the relics of all those wars. Indeed, still utterly vivid in Svoray's mind was the day he had stepped on one of those mines, and now he felt that perhaps it had been a good omen that age had deteriorated it, rendered it harmless, only an innocuous metal casing filled with benign powder. But how many more mines were buried here and how many still had the power to kill and maim?

Peering into those dense forests from their edges, and then venturing a little way into one and then the other, no one, except perhaps Svoray, was filled with overwhelming confidence that the dig that would begin the next morning would end with success. Yes, the landmarks could be made out in triangulations from both forests, the base about 250 yards running in a triangle back into the forests and up about another 250 yards to the ridge. But the forest floor was covered with a foot or more of leaves, marked here and there (but barely distinguishable through the ground cover) with indentations, the remains of hundreds of ancient shell craters and foxholes, dating back to World War I and on to the building of the Maginot Line and then to the arrival of American troops in the winter of 1944–45. Somewhere within one of those two triangulations lay the right foxhole, and somewhere in that foxhole was the pit dug by Sam Nyer and Tommy DeLion in which they buried the purple leather pouch, which must have long since disintegrated, with its forty diamonds. No one doubted that the foxhole was there,

nor that the diamonds were buried in it, but finding that foxhole—recognizing through the thick ground cover which indentations were foxholes and which shell craters, and then the spot
within the right foxhole—would be like searching for a needle
in a haystack, probably more difficult, even though Svoray had
marked what he considered the six most likely foxholes, three in
each woodland.

And there would be the pressure of time. How long would
the searchers have to scour the forests before finding the right
foxhole—even if that were possible, even if it were one of the six
marked by Svoray—before curious residents of the area would
descend on them? And how long would Svoray's diversion, the
hiring of a film crew to film an area away from the dig as part of
his supposed documentary on the vanished dozen American
troops and the diaries they had hidden, keep the curious at a
distance? Svoray had gained permission from local administra-
tors to work on his documentary in these hills, but might not
the lure of a movie being shot on their soil bring out an army of
sightseers? Even as the party stood at the edge of one of the
forests, they were being watched surreptitiously. A farmer on a
tractor was plowing in the cultivated area of the meadow. He
seemed to be ignoring this group of strangers. But Ako Hintzen
and Hammer both noticed that he plowed the same furrow
twice, and then suddenly turned his tractor and headed down
the hill. The prospects for success, for an uninterrupted dig,
grew dimmer the more they considered it.

But if the diamonds were found, what would happen then?
They would have to be moved away from the site without any
delay. For the next half-hour, the group rehearsed the escape
plan. Three cars were lined up on the muddy lane that edged
the forest. Once the diamonds were unearthed, the plan was
that Svoray would race to one of the cars and drive off with a
bodyguard. Other searchers would climb into the other cars and

race after him. One car would stop on the narrow bridge across the Blies, preventing anyone from following them. The other two cars would speed away, one heading east into Germany, the other, with Svoray and the diamonds, racing north toward Luxembourg, where the diamonds would at last be passed on to the man who had once called himself Lieb Zuckerman, who would, it was hoped, turn them to the benefit of the right charities.

An hour later, in a small hotel in Blies Schmeyen, behind the Casablanca disco, Svoray, Kaufman, Hintzen, Berger, and Hammer met in a back room. There was a change of plans. Svoray's strategy to turn the diamonds over to Lieb Zuckerman when—and if—they were found was abandoned. It had not been an idea that appealed greatly to anyone involved, including Svoray. Entrusting the diamonds, whose actual worth nobody knew, to Zuckerman was an incredible risk, given all he had done in his life, all the legal and semilegal activities in which he had been immersed. Could he really be trusted, with no hold over him, no supervision, nothing but his word to rely on, to turn them into money that would be distributed in the right places to the right causes? Even Svoray had his doubts. Zuckerman had even implied that he would have to have something to cover his costs, which seemed to mean that into his pocket would go some of the proceeds. Yet, the alternatives were filled with peril, for everyone in that room, most particularly Svoray. If the diamonds were discovered in the German forest, then few problems might arise. Nobody could imagine that the German government would lay claim to treasure that the Nazis had seized from the Jews in the death camps. But if they were found in the French forest, there would loom the question of the French and their attitude toward anything found on or in their soil. French law, dating back to Napoleon, proclaimed that such treasure, whether found on top of the ground or buried beneath it, belonged to the government. If the diamonds were turned over to that government (someone sarcastically suggested that they ought to be turned over to representatives of the wartime Vichy regime), there was little chance that the proceeds would ever reach the needy, given the example of the Swiss with regard to wartime Jewish bank deposits. Yet the Wiesenthal Center and Yad Vashem had both suggested this as the best course: The diamonds, if found, should be spread out on a table for the world to see, appraised in full view, and then handed over to the French, and when the French resisted distributing the gems or what they brought, the resulting publicity would create something of a firestorm of protest around the world. Svoray told them that a political skirmish was not his aim, nor that of anyone who was with him. Yet Svoray knew he still faced two major potential problems. First, to announce the finding, and display what was found, and *not* hand the gems over to France would mean legal battles extending into the distant future, and a cost, in time, energy, and money, that would exceed everything he had already invested. Second, there would always be the question of the stones' provenance: Who among the millions who perished in the Holocaust had been their original owners? Descendants of Holocaust survivors would no doubt surface and demand that the diamonds be turned over to them. How could anyone determine the validity of such claims? How could anyone distinguish between claims with merit and those with none? The courts would be inundated with lawsuits for decades.

So a new formula had to be developed, one that would circumvent Zuckerman and avoid any potential legal entanglements. Kaufman had been considering alternative possibilities for some time, since the moment he had heard of Zuckerman, and now he had come up with what seemed a viable alternative. He had already set it in motion, even without discussing it with

Svoray. As originally planned, three or four cars would be waiting outside the forest. Once the diamonds were recovered, Kaufman, and not Svoray himself, would take possession of them and climb into the first car, to be driven by Eren Aydogan. Others, including Svoray, would climb into the other cars, one of which would skew across the bridge, blocking it, the other moving after the lead car and then turning in another direction. The lead car, with the diamonds, would head for Frankfurt airport. Kaufman would carry the diamonds onto a plane heading out of Germany for Canada. Once they reached their destination, the next steps would begin. The diamonds would be turned over to an appraiser, who would not be told where they had been found, who would be told nothing about them or their origin. Then they would go to a cutter, who would know only the identity of the appraiser and Kaufman. The cutter would decide which should be cut, which merely cleaned, polished, and shaped, and then slowly and carefully begin to work on them. He would, diamond by diamond, turn them over to someone who would market them, that someone knowing only the identity of the cutter and Kaufman. Once sold, the proceeds would be turned over to a lawyer and a rabbi, who would know only the identity of the seller and Kaufman, and they would then distribute the funds to the needy. Kaufman would be the only person who knew all the links in the chain, because he was the one who had put it together, and, he said, he knew with certainty the integrity of everyone he had recruited, knew that all could be relied on absolutely. It seemed a foolproof plan. Everyone would be protected, only Kaufman aware of each step, since he had set up the chain in advance, but even he would never know to whom the diamonds had been sold nor to whom the money had been given. And his identity would never be revealed.

"It's obvious we won't find the pouch," somebody said.

"Leather disintegrates, and it's probably long gone. If the diamonds are there, they're loose. What if we find only twenty of the diamonds? Maybe the diamonds have scattered and we'll only find twenty. What do we do then?"

"We'll give it twenty more minutes," Hintzen said. "We just can't take chances. We can't stretch time. So we'll search for twenty more minutes, and if we don't find any more, we'll have to be satisfied and get out of there."

Everything, of course, depended on finding the diamonds. And that evening in the back room of the hotel in Blies Schmeyen, only Svoray was brimming with confidence. Necessary as they were, all the planning, all the contingencies might well be nothing more than pipe dreams, and Svoray's show of confidence, whistling past the graveyard.

At eight the next morning, July 10, after a long night of wining and dining in Saar-Louis, east of Saarbrücken, for a pre-victory celebration of sorts, the four-member camera crew from one of the largest TV stations in western Germany, hired by Svoray to film the diversion, and the treasure hunters gathered in the meadow between the twin forests on Kopfberg hill. It was Saturday. Svoray had chosen Saturday as the day for the dig, reasoning that most of the officials and most of the area residents would be on a summer weekend holiday, enjoying their own pleasures and paying little attention to what might be going on in the hills and forests. It was also the Sabbath, and if the scriptures said it was a sin to work on the Sabbath, it was no sin if the work saved lives, and finding the diamonds would certainly save lives and so would be not a sin but a blessing for those who found them.

It had rained during the night, and the sky was still overcast, dark clouds filled with the threat of more rain hanging ominously over the landscape. With Svoray showing the way, the diamond hunters moved into what he considered the most likely of the two forests, heading for the three foxholes he had marked, using his charts and triangulations so that all the landmarks were visible, while he took the camera crew in a different direction to film another location some distance away, out of sight. For the next four hours, Svoray kept racing between the camera crew and the searchers, back and forth, checking and rechecking both, never staying with one for long.

Then the dig began. The leaves were cleared away from the first foxhole. Dirt was shoveled away. Picks dug into the soft, damp soil. Mel Berger climbed into the hole and began to sift through the dirt with his hands, something he would do most of the morning, uncertain, as everyone was, what the diamonds, if found, would look like, what size they might be—perhaps no larger than pebbles. It was an extraordinary sight, a vice president of the William Morris Agency on his hands and knees, mud coating his clothes, searching through muck. He found nothing but a few pebbles in that hole. One of Svoray's diversionary camera crew happened to see him. Later she would say, "I knew then they weren't looking for buried diaries. I didn't know what they were looking for, but it sure wasn't diaries."

It was on to the second foxhole, with the same discouraging result, and then Svoray's third, with no more success. Hintzen and Hammer wandered off and came on a ravine just at the edge of the forest that lay within Svoray's triangulation. Rains through the years had washed away much of the ground, carving out and creating this ravine. If the foxhole had been somewhere there, it and its contents would long since have vanished, been carried far down the hill, and might have ended up anywhere, lost forever. If the odds, someone calculated at that moment, had been ten-to-one against finding the diamonds when the day began, they now loomed at a-thousand-to-one or even more. But it was still early and there were Svoray's other three foxholes in the forest across the meadow. If they didn't pan out, then there were still, by Sam Nyer's estimate of his time in the forest on the hill, probably thirty to forty more foxholes in each forest that might meet all the criteria. Nobody thought the diamonds would be discovered immediately, or even after a few hours, and Svoray had scheduled the dig to last through Saturday and into Sunday, if necessary. If the diamonds weren't unearthed by Sunday evening, then the search would be abandoned and the diamonds left to posterity, or to another search party at some other time. But the idea of digging into sixty or more foxholes over two days—with decreasing prospects for success with each failure, each dig less likely to turn up the diamonds than the one before—was mind boggling.

It was time, then, to move into the second forest across the meadow and explore the three foxholes there that Svoray had marked as his second-best candidates. Svoray continued to divert his camera crew, trying to make sure that if anyone from the area arrived, they'd recognize him as the strange guy who had been wandering the hills for years, talking about making his documentary on the missing dozen, and realize that he was finally doing just that.

Hintzen turned to Hammer. "I can't be in charge of security and make the rest of the decisions at the same time," he said. "Someone else has to make the decisions. You're elected." It was not a job Hammer wanted. He was along, he felt, as an observer, gathering information for the book he would write with Svoray, not as someone suddenly thrust into a leadership role. But now he had no choice.

Something else happened then, something so unexpected that neither Hammer nor Hintzen was prepared for it. Though they had known each other less than two days, at that moment they formed a bond that became a solid and lasting friendship.

For Hammer, at least, it was traumatic. All his life he had studiously avoided crossing the border into Germany. He personally had known no one who had perished in the Holocaust. But when his grandparents had come to the United States from Russia and Austria early in the century, they had left behind scores of relatives, and he knew that those relatives and their descendants must have vanished in gas chambers and crematoriums. If he told himself he rejected the idea of collective guilt, somewhere it pervaded the depths of his mind. And so he had not merely avoided Germany, he had avoided Germans whenever he could, and the contacts he had had with them had been unpleasant and antagonistic. Now he had crossed the physical border into Germany, but more important, in this bonding with Ako Hintzen, he was crossing a border between what had been and what is. He looked at Hintzen. "Even if we don't find the diamonds . . . ," he said, pausing.

And Hintzen finished the thought, ". . . I think we have found something as important, perhaps more important."

"For me," Hammer said.

"For both of us," Hintzen said.

There was no need to say more.

So he and Hintzen wandered together through the second forest, and spotted the foxholes Svoray had designated. They didn't look promising. But they were there, and they might as well be explored. The digging commenced and Berger once more began to sift through the dirt as it was shoveled away, finding only small stones and clumps of mud.

Hintzen and Hammer left the others to ferret around these three foxholes and began to roam around on their own, doing their own search. They moved down toward the tree line, and there they stumbled on two perfectly preserved foxholes, a few hundred feet apart, looking as they must have when they were abandoned half a century before, the leaves and debris on their floors saying they had not been entered or touched within memory. All the landmarks were visible from both. There was just one problem. They were on the tree line, which meant they must have been used by snipers or forward observers, not by scouts who would almost certainly have been dug in well up the hill. Still, these two holes seemed more promising candidates than the three Svoray had marked, so the leaves were cleared away and digging began, Berger in one of the foxholes, Kaufman in the other. They found nothing but dirt and some ancient, empty bottles of beer. To relieve the tension, everyone started to tell jokes.

They weren't very good or very funny, but they cut the tension. The jokes kept on, one after another, each more scatological and obscene than the next.

Hammer and Hintzen watched for a time, then moved off again, climbing the hill toward the crest about 250 yards away, Hintzen walking slowly off to the left, Hammer straight up the hill from a spot almost exactly between the two forward foxholes. Something he didn't know or understand then, or ever—someone would later say it was a higher power that was driving him—compelled him to climb along that straight line, not deviate, dodging the thick growth of trees, struggling through the underbrush and other obstacles. He kept climbing. And then, about fifty feet below the crest, he stopped and froze. Directly before him was a preserved American foxhole, almost as it must have looked in the winter of 1945, except for the mounds of leaves that filled it. Across it lay the remains of a tree trunk, obviously fallen years before and untouched since that day. And just below and to one side of the foxhole was an indentation—a shell crater—it, too, covered with leaves.

Sam Nyer's description of his foxhole and the events of the day he was wounded flooded through Hammer. A shell had exploded near the foxhole just as he had reached it after racing from the forward position where his commanding officer had ordered the artillery barrage and the Germans had begun to return fire. Shrapnel from that shell had smashed into his back and driven him into the foxhole. He had the impression that the shrapnel had also hit a nearby tree and felled it, the trunk falling across the hole right on top of him, and that Tommy had dragged him out from under the remains of that tree. Turning to look down the hill, it was possible, even through the summer leaves that covered the trees, to make out some of the landmarks. At that instant, Hammer was certain that this had to be the right place, that if the diamonds were ever going to be found, they would be found here.

From off to the left, Hintzen called. He had found a couple of other foxholes. Hammer walked over to him and looked at the other foxholes. He shook his head. "I don't think so," he told Hintzen.

"You're making the decisions," Hintzen said.

"I think I've found a better one." They walked back to the foxhole with the tree trunk across it.

Suddenly Svoray appeared. He stared at the foxhole, his face filled with surprise. "I never saw this one," he said. "In all the years, I never saw this one." He stared around. "Can you see the landmarks?" he asked. It was not easy with the leaves covering all the trees between this foxhole and the tree line 200 or more yards down the hill. "Let's make sure," Svoray said. He and Hammer walked down the hill toward the tree line, every step opening the vista, revealing more of the landmarks. They turned and hurried back to the foxhole. Hintzen and the three men in his security team were trying to move the tree trunk away. It may have rotted and partially decomposed after fifty-five years, but it still was large and heavy, and moving it was not easy. The wonder was that Sam Nyer could have survived its impact, especially after being hit by the shrapnel.

One of the security team, Eren, had a rented video camera, and he began to film, though he had never used a video camera before.

Hintzen pulled his gun from his belt pack, handed it to Helmut, and then he and Kaufman climbed into the foxhole and began to clear away the leaves and debris that had been undisturbed for more than half a century. Nyer had said that he and Tommy had dug on the left side of their foxhole. But did he mean the left side facing the German positions, or the left side facing the crest of the hill? No one was certain. The decision was to try the left side facing down the hill toward the German lines. Barbed wire suddenly emerged from beneath the first layer of dirt, American barbed wire ringing the edge of the foxhole. Nyer had said that he and Tommy, like a lot of other GIs, had ringed their foxhole with barbed wire around the edges as a protection. The wire was rusted, barbs obviously loaded with every imaginable disease, from tetanus to the plague. The wire was handled carefully, nobody touching the barbs, and tossed to one side. Svoray said, "I think I ought to take a piece and send it to Sam as a souvenir." Nobody took that idea seriously, and Svoray thought better of it.

Once the foxhole was cleared of the debris, Hintzen and Kaufman started to dig into the dirt on that side with small picks. "Don't dig straight down," Hammer said. "Remember, when they were digging it was February. The ground was frozen. So their tools must have slid off at oblique angles, which means they were digging outside the perimeter. So dig at an angle."

As the soil was cleared away, large slabs of rock appeared, looking as though a wall had been erected along the sides. Hintzen pulled away the rocks. Behind was an opening, like a small vault. He reached in. Nothing.

There wasn't room for two diggers on the left side. Kaufman

fell backward across the foxhole, turned over, and after a few minutes started digging obliquely into the other side, the left side facing the crest of the hill, excavating out from the perimeter. He cleared away the dirt, opening a small hole in the side of the foxhole. Suddenly he stopped, looked around. "Somebody give me the small pick," he said. Nobody moved. "Dammit, give me the small pick." Chalid grabbed the pick and handed it to him. He dug some more, then pulled away a small piece of barbed wire, about a foot in length, that had been stretched at an angle across the small hole he was opening. Carefully, he cleared away more dirt, and the hole grew bigger. Dropping the pick, he reached his hand, covered with a rubber glove, into the muddy chamber.

He had said at the beginning of the morning, "If we find the diamonds, I sure as hell don't want to be the one who finds them, who touches them." Maybe they were cursed, as Sam Nyer believed, or maybe not, but they certainly hadn't brought any good luck to anyone who had ever touched them. And he didn't want to be the one. But now he had no choice. It was as though someone had assigned a task to everyone there, a task that no one wanted but that had to be accepted.

His gloved hand groped around the hole. Suddenly, his face changed. He froze for an instant. His voice was strained, rasping. He turned and looked at the seven team members gathered around the foxhole, Eren filming it all with his video camera. "You're not going to believe this," he said.

And then his hand came out. It held a diamond. It was bigger than any diamond anyone in that group had ever seen. It was coated with mud, but part of it was visible, and in that part could be seen a light that glowed, as though life were returning to it after years in the darkness. It was, somebody said later, a real Life Diamond.

The time was precisely noon on this gray, overcast Saturday.

Berger later said that the sight of those diamonds was over-whelming, and he felt that this was of one of the two most important events of his life, the other, the birth of his daughter.

At that moment, with the emergence of the first diamond into the light after such a long time in darkness, images flooded the minds of those witnessing the discovery, disturbing visions of the torment of Pal Abraham and Dorit Klotz and all the lost children of Birkenau, of Jack Eisner and Joseph Uberkleider and all the dead but never-forgotten children of Majdanek, of all the children in all the death camps who had been forced to search, if not for these diamonds, then for other diamonds. And with those images came the utter realization, if there had been any doubt, that the diamonds belonged to none of these searchers on this July morning, could belong to no one. No mat-ter what riches these diamonds were worth in money, no matter what they might bring, it would never come close to matching what they had cost, in torment, in agony, in blood, in death.

Hintzen started to reach for a bucket, but before he could grasp it, Helmut was thrusting his gun back at him, and simul-taneously Chalid grabbed the bucket and passed it to Hintzen. Hintzen put away the gun, grabbed the bucket and filled it with water, took the diamond, and dropped it into the bucket. Kauf-man reached back into the hole, came out with three more large, mud-covered diamonds, and handed them to Hintzen, who added them to the bucket. The water began to turn brown, opaque. Kaufman's hand kept reaching into the hole, coming out with more diamonds, three, four, five at a time, all large, all coated with mud, all glowing with life inside, all added to the bucket, the water now sludge. One among the many caught and held the eye. Inside was not a white glow, nor a blue one. This one had a red fire blazing within, or, it occurred to the searchers, was it blood? It glowed for only a moment before the diamond disappeared into the bucket.

Svoray was staring, rigid. Then he said, "I want to hold one."
"No," Hintzen said.

"I want to hold one," Svoray repeated. "I have to hold one."
He reached. Hintzen reached into the bucket, took out one large
diamond, and handed it to Svoray. The Israeli who had spent so
many years searching for these stones held it in his hand for just
an instant before Hintzen retrieved it and dropped it back into
the muddy water.

Svoray began to sob uncontrollably, hysterically. He spun
around and stumbled up the hill, put his arms around a tree,
and kept sobbing. "I'm sorry, I'm sorry, I'm acting like a baby."
But he couldn't stop crying. For a decade he had been anticipat-
ing this moment. It had dominated all his thinking, all his
actions, his whole life. He had mortgaged his past, his present,
and his future to reach this goal. Now it had arrived. Yet it
would bring with it none of the fortune he had originally
dreamed of. It would not provide the means even to clear away
part of the mountainous debt he had accumulated in his search.
But at that moment, and even later, that meant nothing. He had
done what had seemed, through all the years, the impossible. He
had led the way to the treasure, and the treasure would be used
not for his benefit, but for the benefit of many he did not know
and would never know, who would never thank him, would
never know what he had done for them. It was enough.

He kept holding the tree and crying. Someone went to him,
grasped his shoulder, said, "It's okay. We all understand. Be
proud, Yaron. You're responsible for a miracle."

Svoray released his hold on the tree and stumbled back down
the hill to stand over the foxhole.

More diamonds kept coming from the hole, kept dropping
into the bucket. No one was counting. Everybody was just
watching, unable to do anything else. And then there were no
more. Kaufman's hand scrabbled frantically around the hole.

There was nothing more to find. Somewhere in there were the other items Sam Nyer had deposited, but they must have been buried deeper, or been washed away in some torrent. The diamonds had remained.

"Give me the rubber glove," Hintzen said then. There was no response. "Dammit," Hintzen repeated, "give me the rubber glove." Finally, Kaufman understood. He pulled off the glove and handed to Hintzen. Hintzen passed it back to Kaufman. "Hold it open," he said, and began to pull the diamonds out of the sludge in the bucket. They were cleaner now, the life within them more visible, glowing, dancing, and in some there was color—blue, more red ones, an orange one, a pink stone, others. And then the count began—one, two, and on and on until the count reached thirty-nine. Hintzen's hand fished, swirling the mud, finding nothing, and then he grinned, his hand emerging, holding one last diamond, the smallest, a little larger than a thumbnail. Someone later dubbed it the runt of the litter. "Forty."

They were all there, in the rubber glove.

"I have to hold them," Svoray said.

Hintzen reached out and took Svoray's maroon baseball cap off Svoray's head, the logo for the University of Nebraska Cornhuskers on its front, held it open, and handed it to Svoray. Hintzen took the rubber glove and dumped the diamonds into the cap. Svoray was rigid, his face changing color, flooding with emotion, elation, amazement, relief, perhaps even a sense of finality, that it was over. He held the cap filled with diamonds and barely glanced at them. There they remained for less than a minute in Svoray's hands. Hintzen pulled his belt pack from his waist, took the cap from Svoray, and poured the diamonds into the pack. It bulged. He closed it tightly.

But Kaufman wanted to keep searching, seeking the other

items Sam Nyer and Tommy had buried. "Give him ten minutes," Hintzen said.

"Twenty," Hammer said. "That's what we agreed on."

"Okay, twenty," Hintzen said. "But no more. We've got all forty. We have to get out of here."

Kaufman continued to explore the cavern, digging through it, but finding nothing more. If the other trinkets were there, if the letters from Nyer's father still existed, they were buried deeper, or had been washed somewhere down the hill, and they would remain for some other treasure hunter. After about five minutes, the search ended. It was a little after twelve-fifteen. Kaufman—his clothes, his hair, his face coated with mud—climbed out of the foxhole. He, Hintzen, Svoray, and two of Hintzen's crew moved rapidly out of the forest toward the waiting cars. Hintzen ordered Svoray into one of the cars.

"No," Svoray said, his voice, his manner confused, stunned. "I want to walk. I want to walk home to Mikhal."

"Get in the car, Yaron," Hintzen said.

"No," Svoray repeated. "I want to walk home to Mikhal."

"What?" Hintzen said. "You're going to walk to Israel? You think you can walk on water? Get into the car." And he forced Svoray into one of the waiting cars.

Berger, Hammer, and Helmut stayed behind, gathering the shovels, the picks, the blue plastic sheets, everything they could find that would indicate that anybody had been there.

"Should we cover up the digging?"

"The hell with it."

Carrying all the tools, they left the forest, went to the remaining car, and drove off, down the muddy lane and down the hill toward the Blies River. A car was skewed across the bridge, blocking it. The other cars had passed by, carrying the diamonds wherever they were heading.

Back at the hotel in Blies Schmeyen, they waited for the others to return. They wandered around, amazed and still trying to believe what had been accomplished, laughing strange laughter, not of victory or success but of something else, something that could not be explained, as so much that had happened that day was beyond understanding or explanation. The camera crew arrived back from the hill and began to pack up their things, realizing that the day's shoot was finished, earlier than expected, that, indeed, the searchers must have found what they were looking for, and it wasn't diaries, and so they would not be needed again.

Then Hintzen and Svoray appeared. Kaufman and the diamonds were on their way.

That night in Frankfurt, Hintzen, Svoray, Berger, and Hammer waited for word that the diamonds had safely reached their destination. It did not come. And Hintzen ordered that there were to be no phone calls to anyone until that word arrived. So they waited.

In the morning, there was still no news. Still shaken, unable to fully grasp what had been accomplished, Svoray insisted that he had to call his wife in Israel. Hintzen relented. The call was made, the conversation circuitous, but Svoray's wife understood enough. She couldn't believe what she was hearing, insisted that Hintzen, Berger, and Hammer all confirm. It was enough for the moment. She would hear the details later.

Svoray made a second call, with Hintzen's approval. He called the hotel in Luxembourg where Lieb Zuckerman was waiting. There had been a change of plans, he explained, and there would be no need for Zuckerman's help. He could almost hear Zuckerman shrug through the phone line. "So be it," Zuckerman said.

But still there was no news from Kaufman. Hintzen and Svoray headed for Cologne, Hintzen's home, to wait there. Berger and Hammer caught a train for Paris.

When Berger and Hammer arrived that evening, they called Hintzen. "I just got word," Hintzen said. "The word is, 'The kid is home safe. The grandkids are already with their new parents.'"

But even this last segment of the journey had been long and traumatic. With Chalid at the wheel, Kaufman, with the forty diamonds nestled in Hintzen's gun pack, had sped the two hours to Frankfurt, stopping only once at a gas station to wash the mud off himself and change into fresh clothes. At the airport in Frankfurt, he walked into one of the shops and bought a cosmetic case. In the first-class lounge, he surreptitiously transferred the diamonds into it, then stowed the case in his luggage, which he checked through to Toronto as a priority first-class passenger. He was not about to carry the gems in a carry-on satchel that might be examined. While waiting for the plane to depart, he made a couple of calls to Canada. The first was to a girl for a date that night. The second call was to the contact who was to meet him in the washroom at the airport in Toronto and who would take possession of the diamonds so they could start on their final journey.

As he approached the departure gate, he was stopped momentarily and questioned about what he had been doing and why his stay had been so brief. It was an anxious moment, but his explanation that this had been a quick business trip was accepted, and he moved through the gate and onto the plane.

Once on board, nervous and exhausted, he fell into a deep sleep even before takeoff and slept for the entire flight, waking only once to find stewardesses standing over him anxiously, wondering if he was still alive.

Arriving in Toronto, he expected that his luggage would appear within moments with the rest of the priority first-class baggage. It didn't. He waited. The first-class carousel emptied and still his suitcase did not arrive. The carousel with the rest of the plane's luggage began to turn and he waited nervously. Still no suitcase. The carousel emptied, stopped, then started to turn again, and at last his suitcase appeared. He grabbed it and moved toward immigration. On the plane, he had filled out the customs card, stating that he had purchased nothing while abroad. The immigration official took the card. "Usually," Kaufman said later, "they take a quick look and wave you through. This time, the guy took the card and studied it closely."

"Where are you coming from?"

"Frankfurt."

"What were you doing there?"

"Quick business trip."

The customs guard continued to study the declaration form. Kaufman was sure that he was going to ask to examine the suitcase. What would Kaufman tell him if he looked in the cosmetic case and found the stones? He decided he'd say they were just some things he found while hiking, and hope that the answer would suffice. Another minute, which seemed like an hour, and then the customs guard waved him through.

Kaufman headed for the rendezvous, the men's washroom. The man he had called from Frankfurt was waiting. They exchanged prearranged signals. Kaufman opened his suitcase, removed the cosmetic case, and handed it to him. It was the last he would ever see of the diamonds.

When he arrived home, he tried to call Frankfurt with the news. He couldn't get through. He picked up his girl and they drove north to his country home, went to sleep, and slept for hours. He called again when he woke up, and this time made contact.

There was something else as well. Earlier that Sunday, Helmut returned to the forest with his wife and daughter to make sure that nothing had been left behind. No one had told him to, no one had even suggested it. He simply took it upon himself to do this, something that had to be done. As he treaded through the leaves and underbrush, he suddenly discovered a small white slip of paper, a map of the area on one side, on the other the names, addresses, and phone numbers of those who had been there. He retrieved it quickly and shoved it into his pocket. A few minutes later, he noticed that gendarmes had appeared in the forest. They were moving through it and were gathering around the foxhole. What they were doing there or what they were looking for they never said. They saw Helmut and quickly approached. "What are you doing here?" they demanded.

Helmut replied that he was merely taking his family for a hike in these publicly owned woods.

They heard him out and sent him on his way. Then they spent the next several hours searching the area.

A week later, Svoray tried to reach Sam Nyer. Nobody was home. He left word on the answering machine for Nyer to call him. A week passed, and then the call was returned.

"I wanted to tell you," Nyer said, "I wasn't home when you called because I was in the hospital. I had a mild heart attack."

"When?"

"July 10," Nyer said. "I'm okay now."

"Sit down," Svoray said. "I have something to tell you and I don't want you to get upset."

"I'm sitting."

"We found the diamonds. On July 10."

It took moments for that to sink in. "I'm elated," he said at last. "I'm so happy." Then, "Yaron, do you remember what you promised me a long time ago, when you started this search?"

"Yes, I remember." Actually, Svoray didn't remember, couldn't recall any promise he had made.

"You promised that if you found the diamonds, you'd give them to charity, you wouldn't keep them because they don't belong to you. They don't belong to anyone."

"I made that promise," Svoray said, "and I want you to know, the diamonds are all going to charity."

"I'm glad about that," Nyer said. "You're blessed, and God will reward you."

In the days and weeks following the discovery of the diamonds, unanswered and unanswerable questions danced in the minds of some of the searchers. They had uncovered forty diamonds that the Nazis had looted from those they exterminated. Forty. But how many more diamonds, uncut Life Diamonds as well as thousands of cut ones, had the Nazis seized? Of those, how many had ever been recovered? Some had obviously made another journey, in the pockets of escaping Wehrmacht officers and SS officials and other Nazi overlords, to South America or the Middle East or other destinations where the leaders and underlings of the fallen Reich had fled. These diamonds had obviously provided the means for their prosperous survival in hiding. But had they brought luck and good fortune? Or had they, too, been cursed? Had possession of them led their possessors to spend the rest of their lives on the run, in disguise, always looking over their shoulders in fear of pursuers, in fear of retribution? And how many continued to remain, hidden in safe-deposit boxes and other repositories around the world, or buried in other holes in other forests and fields, undiscovered, still waiting? No one would ever know.

For these forty Life Diamonds, the circle had finally closed and the journey had come to an end. The diamonds dug from the earth at the mines in South Africa, transported to London and then to Amsterdam and Antwerp, some bought by agents of wealthy Jews in Eastern Europe as insurance against disaster, ferreted out from the prisoners' garments by the soon-to-be-exterminated children in the Nazi death camps, sent to KZ Vught, appraised there by Lieb Zuckerman, placed in a purple leather pouch and carried by the SS to that secret depository in a small town near Strasbourg, or carried in that pouch from Berlin supposedly to KZ Vught but diverted, liberated by Sam Nyer and Tommy DeLion and buried by them on a freezing February night in a foxhole in Alsace—these stones had seen more than enough misery and torture and death to fill a hundred, a thousand lifetimes. Sam Nyer believed, as did others, that they were cursed, and would profit no man, would enrich no person. And so the curse would now be lifted, as they heal the destitute and ravaged children of our time, the ultimate victims of man's inhumanity to man.

For the eight men who had made their own journey in search of the diamonds, there was something else, too. During the brief time they had been in the forests on the hill, their lives had changed. They were no longer the men they had been just twenty-four hours before. They had done something that, when they began, seemed nearly impossible. And they had done it without thought or even hope that they would profit by their act. As the diamonds had emerged, none considered taking even one. In a real sense, they were ennobled. They were uplifted by the realization that, in a world driven by self-aggrandizement, it was still possible to do an unselfish deed, to do good. It would remain with them for the rest of their lives.

During the months after the discovery of the diamonds and their immediate disappearance, those who had been on the hill that July day were subjected to repeated and almost identical questions, to which they gave nearly identical answers.

Where are the diamonds now?

We have no idea.

Aren't you curious? Don't you want to know?

No. It was enough that we found them. And sent them on their way.

How large were those diamonds?

Very large. The largest any of us had ever seen.

How much were they worth?

We have no idea. Only an appraiser would know.

How can you be sure they have gone where you wanted, that they will do what you desired?

We can't be sure. We can only hope. But it was enough to have found them and sent them on their way.

Why didn't you keep at least one for each of you?

That had never entered the mind of anyone who was there. To understand, you would have to have been there, found them, seen them, and sensed from where they had come and what they had cost.

Yaron Svoray had given eleven years of his life to this quest and now had seen it come to fruition. The questions would remain, and there was little he or anyone else could do about them but tell the truth, even if some would not believe it. But now his long and often lonely and tortuous journey, one that so often seemed impossible, was over. At its end, he and his friends had found those stones and had washed them clean of the blood that had permeated them for so long.

Appendix A: Cursed Diamonds

From the time when diamonds were first discovered, men have believed that evil curses hang over these precious stones. The first recorded legend of a cursed diamond, though, is that of the fabulous Koh-i-Nor. A brilliant, flashing stone of more than 600 carats, found on a riverbank in northern India, it was embedded as the third eye in a statue of Shiva in the village of Thanesar. According to legend, as long as it remained the third eye of Shiva, it would cause no harm. But at some point, Shiva lost his third eye and the Koh-i-Nor wound up as one of the prized possessions of the rajah of Malawah, who handed it down to his successors. But once removed from the protection of Shiva, the diamond's curse was set in motion. Plots and counterplots roiled the palace until, in 1526, Babur, a descendant of Tamerlane, invaded and conquered India and was presented with the diamond as an act of submission. It was then embedded in the design of the fabled Peacock Throne, where it remained until the Persian ruler, Nadir Shah, conquered India in 1739. But the Koh-i-Nor had vanished. It had been surreptitiously pried from the throne by the deposed ruler, Mohammed Shah, who hid the diamond in his turban. Nadir Shah was furious. Then Mohammed Shah's neglected wife, or concubine, depending on the story, revealed the secret hiding place. Rather than start another war in an attempt to recover the diamond, Nadir Shah came up with what seemed like a foolproof plan. He held a feast where, custom had it, turbans were exchanged. Mohammed Shah had no choice but to hand over his, and when Nadir Shah unwrapped it, out fell the huge diamond. "Koh-i-Nor!" he reportedly shouted when he saw it, meaning "Mountain of Light." And then he carried it back to Persia.

Almost as soon as he returned home, he was assassinated. His grandson, Shah Runk, who took the diamond for his own, was kidnapped by raiders and the ransom demanded was the diamond. It was taken by Ahmed Shah, whose family managed to retain possession of it for two generations, until family feuding erupted over it. One of Ahmed's grandsons, Shuja, deposed his brother, Zaman, and had his eyes torn out when Zaman refused to reveal the whereabouts of the gem. Shuja found it anyway, but almost immediately he was ousted and sought refuge with the Sikh ruler of Punjab, Ranjit Singh, who demanded the Koh-i-Nor in exchange for his protection. Finally, in 1849, the British seized the Mountain of Light when they conquered Punjab. They presented it to Queen Victoria, who had it cut to 108.93 carats. Since that time, it has adorned British monarchs on state occasions, and most of the time is on display in the Tower of London with the other crown jewels.

The curse of the Koh-i-Nor is certainly not unique. Mention the names of the most fabulous diamonds and there are reverberations of assassinations, murders, suicides, disasters of all kinds, some real, most fabrications, though accepted as gospel truth.

There is the 140.5-carat Regent (cut and mounted from the original 410-carat stone found in the Partial mine along India's Krishna River), stolen by a slave who offered it to a British sea captain in exchange for passage to freedom. The sea captain murdered the slave, threw him overboard, then sold the stone to an Indian merchant and promptly squandered the proceeds on wine, women, and song, and finally, beset by dementia, hanged himself. In 1702, the diamond was purchased for £20,400 by Thomas Pitt, governor of Madras and grandfather of the later British Prime Minister William Pitt. But rumors spread that Pitt had acquired the stone by nefarious means, and for years he was haunted by fears that he would somehow lose it or it would be stolen. He never spent two nights under the same roof, adopted numerous disguises, told no one his whereabouts, and refused to show the stone even to close friends. He tried to sell it to every European sovereign. All refused to buy it until, finally, in 1717, Philippe d'Orleans, regent of France for the child King Louis XVI, after much hesitation over the price, bought it for the monarch for £135,000, the highest price ever paid for a jewel to that time. The duke named the stone the Regent. Disaster followed disaster for the subsequent owners until the Regent disappeared, along with a horde of other diamonds and precious gems, during the night of September 17, 1792, a thief apparently making away with it and hiding it in the attic of a house in Paris, where it was discovered several years later. It found its way to Napoleon, who used it as collateral for loans to finance his rise to power and his conquests. Once Napoleon was sent to Elba, the Regent became the property of the French state, one of the crown jewels. In 1940, when the Nazis entered Paris, the Regent was rushed out of the city and hidden in the plaster behind a white marble fireplace in the Château Chambord. The war over, it was returned to the city, and today it is displayed in the Galerie d'Apollon at the Louvre.

The 189.6-carat Orlov and the Great Mogul, according to legend, were intimately tied, twins, each shaped like half a pigeon's egg. In the mid-seventeenth century, the Great Mogul vanished and, with its disappearance, the story of the Orlov began.

Found in the Kollur deposits in India, the Great Mogul weighed more than 787 carats. The Mogul ruler, Aurangzeb, who came into possession of it, turned it over to Hortenzio Borgia in Italy to cut and shape. According to Jean Baptiste Tavernier, the French jeweler who traveled widely in India and carried back to Europe fabulous diamonds during the seventeenth century, Borgia made a mess of the job, nearly destroying the diamond, and the enraged Aurangzeb fined him 100,000 rupees. Still, there was enough of the Great Mogul left to make it a prized possession of the Mogul ruler, but when his empire was conquered by Persia, the stone vanished and it has never been heard of since.

It was then that the Orlov made its appearance. No one is certain whether it was the twin, the other half of the Great Mogul, as some believe, or whether it was cut from the Great Mogul—or even if it was a separate stone altogether. But the legend surrounding it, like all legends of great and cursed diamonds, is both melodramatic and tangled. Set in the eye of a statue of Vishnu in a Hindu temple on a river island at Srirangam in Madras, according to one story, a French soldier, who had fought in the eighteenth-century French-English battles over Tiruchirapalli, heard of the diamond and was determined to see it and, if possible, possess it. He went to the temple, ingratiated himself with the priests, and took on the role of acolyte. He spent several years in this way, until he managed to gain access to the innermost chamber, where the image of Vishnu towered. He pried the diamond from the statue and fled to Madras, where he sold it to a sea captain for £2,000, a bargain for the seaman and a disaster for the soldier, considering the time and effort it had taken him to steal the stone. When the sea captain reached London, he sold it to a Jew for £12,000. The Jew sold it to a Persian named Khojeh who carried it to Amsterdam, where he couldn't find a buyer until he finally came upon Count Grigori Grigorievich Orlov, a one-time favorite of Catherine the Great, who was looking for a way to reingratiate himself with the empress.

Another, and even more colorful, story revolves around an Afghan soldier serving with the Persians during the sacking of Delhi in 1739. The Afghan stole the diamond from the statue of Vishnu and made his way to Basra where he offered an Armenian merchant, one Grigori Safras, a pile of precious stones, but before Safras had an opportunity to make an offer, the Armenian fled to Baghdad, where he sold his loot to a Jewish merchant. Safras followed in hot pursuit, found the Jewish merchant, and tried to persuade him to sell the gems. The merchant refused. So Safras had him poisoned, made off with the jewels, and headed for Amsterdam, where he set up shop as a diamond dealer.

In 1775, he had a customer for his most marvelous of diamonds, the eye of Vishnu. The customer was Count Grigori Grigorievich Orlov. Determined to win Catherine back, Orlov had journeyed to Amsterdam to buy her the best diamond he could find. He found it at Safras's shop and bought it for 400,000 rubles, carried it back to Russia, and presented it to the empress. Catherine gave it his name, the Orlov diamond, set it in the imperial scepter just below the golden eagle—and then threw Orlov aside again, this time in favor of Field Marshal Grigori Alexandrovich Potemkin. The despondent Orlov, all his plans in ruins, went mad and was committed to an asylum, where he died in 1783.

Of all the cursed diamonds, though, none has captured the public imagination more than the Great Blue diamond, which later became known as the Hope, a magnificent 44.5-carat gem.

According to one, apocryphal, story, Tavernier, during one of his journeys to India, saw the stone in a statue of the god Rama Sita, and tore it from its mounting. He carried it back to France and sold it to Louis XIV; almost immediately after the sale, however, he went bankrupt and had to sail again to India to recoup his fortune. But instead of amassing a new fortune, he met his death, devoured, one story says, by mad dogs, or by a tiger, according to another legend. Back in France, King Louis wore the diamond once and died within days.

Another apocryphal version says the Great Blue was sold not to Louis XIV but to his finance minister, Nicolas Fouquet, who was promptly stripped of the title and thrown into prison, where he remained for the rest of his life. Then King Louis gave the stone to the Marquise de Montespan, who subsequently fell deathly ill. King Louis XV gained possession of the diamond and let his mistress, the Countess du Barry, wear it. The result: She was executed in 1793. Louis XVI wore it as an ornament, as did his queen, Marie Antoinette, and her friend, the Princess de Lambelle. All went to the guillotine.

Pure invention. None of these events ever happened, though they were widely believed, and are still accepted as fact by many. Tavernier did not tear the stone from a statue of the god; it was found in a tributary of the Coleroon River. Tavernier was not devoured by mad dogs or tigers, but died in Moscow of a common cold at the age of eighty-four. When he sold the diamond to Louis XIV, Fouquet had long since fallen from favor and had been in prison for seven years. Louis, who was generous to his mistresses and allowed them to wear some of his jewels, jealously guarded the most precious crown jewels. And he did not die after wearing it, but lived another forty-six years after acquiring it.

If the tales of the curse of the Great Blue are pure fiction, what is the truth? In 1672, after buying the diamond from Tavernier, Louis turned the diamond over to a man named Pitou, the diamond cutter to the monarch, who cut it from its original

112 carats into a heart-shaped gem of 67.5 carats. In succeeding years, Louis wore it several times, as did his successors, Louis XV and Louis XVI. In September 1792, during the French Revolution, it was stolen with the rest of the crown jewels from the Garde-Meuble National and wound up in the hands of a man named Cadet-Guillot who carried it to London, where it was recut into a gem of 44.5 carats, and was then purchased either by Queen Maria Luisa of Spain or by the Duke of Brunswick.

In 1830, it was sold at auction in London for £18,000 to the banker, Henry Philip Hope, who gave it his name. And then the stories of the cursed Hope diamond multiplied. The Hopes, rumors went, died in poverty. A Russian prince bought the Hope and that same evening shot his mistress, Mademoiselle Ladrue, a Folies-Bergère dancer. The Sultan Abdul Hamid II was the next owner. He presented it to his favorite, Zobeida, and then killed her. The next owner was the American millionaire Edward B. McLean, owner of the *Washington Post*, who went down with the *Titanic*. His granddaughter committed suicide after wearing it, and his widow lost her fortune and also took her own life.

It seemed that any disaster that befell anyone even remotely connected to the Hope diamond was blamed on the curse that had descended over the stone. True? No. In fact, in 1908, in order to clear away mounting debts, Lord Hope sold the Hope to Sultan Abdul Hamid II, who killed no one, certainly not a favorite. A year after he acquired the Hope, the sultan was deposed and, in 1911, he sold the diamond to Pierre Cartier, the famous Paris jeweler. McLean bought it from him soon thereafter and presented it to his wife, who called it a good-luck charm because of its name and wore it until her death in 1947. Two years later, the jeweler Harry Winston bought it for $179,920, kept it for ten years, and then, on November 8, 1958, sent it by parcel post in a small package with $2.44 in postage and insurance of $151 to the Smithsonian Institute, where it rests to this day in a special bulletproof display case.

The curse of the Hope diamond, then, is nothing more than a myth, yet the belief in the curse is real, as is the belief that the great diamonds of the world all carry curses. People still hold fast to those beliefs no matter what facts contradict them.

Appendix B: Rhodes Versus Barnato

Though his dream of controlling the South African diamond fields was dead, with the victory of Cecil Rhodes, Barney Barnato was hardly ruined financially. He was compelled to sell his shares in the various diamond corporations to Rhodes, a sale that made him even richer than he had been before. But the money did nothing to assuage the bitterness he felt at his defeat by the man he detested above all others, and who detested him, both as a rival and as a Jew. He sank into a deep depression, and on June 13, 1897, while sailing to England, he leaped from the ship to his death in the sea. His body was recovered and carried to England. There, two hundred carriages, in one the Lord Mayor of London, in others representatives of British nobility, followed the hearse to the Jewish cemetery in Wileseden. The most conspicuous absentee among the mourners was Cecil Rhodes. "I suppose you thought this would affect me and I should not sleep," Rhodes said when told of Barnato's suicide. "Why should you imagine that I would be in the least affected?"

Rhodes's victory allowed De Beers to inaugurate the strategy that would ultimately bring order to what was becoming a chaotic diamond market. The fabulous discoveries in the Kimberly fields and elsewhere in South Africa, leading to an unchecked influx of vast quantities of rough diamonds into the European centers in Antwerp and Amsterdam, and now London as well, caused diamond prices to tumble sharply, though not as sharply as they might have had the discoveries been made a century earlier. The growing prosperity in the United States, England, and Western Europe opened new markets for diamonds, made them prized possessions. But even with that, falling prices posed a danger. Rhodes came up with a strategy that dealt with the danger. Diamond output would now be regulated and limited, the glut would cease, and prices would inevitably rise to new levels. The creation of the De Beers monopoly had begun.

But Rhodes did not live long enough to see the fruits of his labor. He died on March 26, 1902, at his South African estate, isolated and friendless. At his death he was the most hated man in South Africa. His manner had been imperious. He thought no man his peer, no man even close to his equal. He was a racist who dreamed of a world dominated by an Anglo-Saxon elite, to whom all would be subservient. His treatment of South African blacks, whom he considered the lowest of men, had been cruel in the extreme, which might have won the approval of the Boers; but he was contemptuous of them, as he was of anyone and everyone with whom he came in contact—ordinary miners on whom he depended in many ways for his fortune, business associates, and rivals. He had named a country for himself, Rhodesia, convinced it would last as his monument; yet with the end of British colonialism, its name was erased, and the country became Zimbabwe. All that remains of Rhodes in most memories are the Oxford scholarships he created. He was, *Le Temps* wrote, a man "without religion, without love, and without ideals; he lived only for his schemes, and enjoyed life only as a cannonball enjoys space, traveling to its aim blindly and spreading ruin on its way. He was a great man, no doubt—a man who rendered immense service to his country, but humanity is not much indebted to him."

There were those, looking over the ultimate tragedies of both Cecil Rhodes and Barney Barnato, who said that both men were, finally, the victims of the curse of diamonds.

Appendix C: Coming Home

It was not until early in 2002, fifty-seven years after Tommy DeLion's death, that Sam Nyer learned that his friend had been buried neither in a military cemetery in France among thousands of other American soldiers killed in the two world wars, nor in a dusty grave on some Indian reservation in the Southwest, probably New Mexico, where, Nyer was convinced, he had been born and grown up. Rather, his body had been sent home and interred in a cemetery in Morrill, Nebraska. "It can't be true," Nyer said.

And that day Nyer learned something else, as well. Tommy DeLion was not, as Nyer and the other soldiers in his company believed, a Native American. If an Indian at all, he was descended from a tribe in Mexico. He was the son of migrant farmworkers who had drifted across the border from Mexico in search of work, following the sun and the seasons and the crops north and south. Tommy was born in Texas in 1925, one stop on his family's journey north of the border in search of work. A brother, Oliver, and a sister followed in the next years.

By the late 1920s or early 1930s, the family came to rest in Morrill, Nebraska, a small farming town of fewer than two thousand inhabitants in the southwest corner of the state, close to the border with Wyoming. The nearest city of any size was

Scottsbluff. The family homestead in Morrill was a migrant workers' shack; no electricity, no running water, no plumbing, and, of course, no telephone or radio—none of the amenities that most people would later take for granted. It was in Morrill that Tommy grew up, went to school, found what little work there was. He was a small, quiet youngster who was rarely in any trouble, who made little impression on those he came into contact with.

In late 1943, just turned eighteen, he went to Scottsbluff, enlisted in the Army, and was sent to a camp in Texas for basic training. His family would see him only once more, when he returned on leave, carrying with him a three-dimensional, bronze, embossed portrait of himself, a photograph of his head superimposed over a figure in uniform with an American flag on one side. His mother placed the photo on the mantel, and there it would remain.

Leave over, he was shipped out to the war in Europe. His family never heard from him again. He never wrote letters, never communicated in any way. The next word they had was the telegram from the War Department in May 1945. "We regret to inform you that your son, Thomas DeLion, has been killed in action." His mother would say, "I sent my son to war, I saw him once, and then they sent his body home in a box."

A year and a month later, the casket containing Tommy's body was shipped home, carried to the cemetery in Morrill, escorted by two Army officers. The family gathered for the funeral; everyone except Tommy's brother, Oliver. He was away that day, and when he learned the news that his brother's body had reached Morrill and the funeral would be that day, he tried to get back in time. But his bus was four hours late and so he missed the burial.

As the casket rested above the open grave before being lowered into its final resting place, Tommy's medals—a bronze star, a purple heart, a decoration from the French government, more—were displayed on the closed coffin. No one told the family what he had done to earn those medals. That would remain a mystery to them all through the years that followed. They were sure he had done noble things, that he had been a hero, a son, a brother, a relative to be proud of. Exactly what he had done, they didn't know, and didn't ask.

Tommy's mother requested that the coffin be opened so she could take a last look at her son, make sure that the body inside was really his. The request was refused. In the years to come, his mother grew increasingly convinced that the reason the coffin had not been opened was because it was not Tommy's body inside, that he was still alive somewhere and would eventually turn up.

A few years later, the family left Morrill, traveled nearly five hundred miles south, and came to rest in Ulysses, Kansas, the county seat of Grant County, a town of fewer than ten thousand souls. They took with them all they could or all they wanted to keep. Somehow, during the move, Tommy's medals were mislaid and never found. But not that bronzed portrait. Once in the new home, that picture found an honored place on the mantel, where it remains to this day. Family members would point to it and say Tommy had been a hero who had died for his country. It made such an impression on future generations that six of his later relatives would pursue careers in the military services. In Morrill, nobody but the local Veterans of Foreign Wars, who tended the graves of fallen veterans, ever came to see Tommy's final resting place. The family was gone, settled in Kansas, dispersed to other locales, upwardly mobile, moving into the middle class, and enjoying the American dream. Nobody had any desire or reason to return to Morrill.

Over the years, as he abandoned his obsession and his search for the forty cursed diamonds—leaving that to Yaron Svoray—

Sam Nyer kept thinking back to his friend. Somehow, he told himself, he would find Tommy's grave and say final farewells to the man he considered his closest friend, come to terms with his death, put, he said, closure on that part of his life. Once his son traveled to the Southwest and, at Nyer's insistence, went in search of Tommy DeLion's grave in New Mexico and Arizona. It was not to be found.

Then, during the writing of this book, a researcher discovered that the search for Tommy's grave had been in the wrong place, just as Svoray's initial search for the diamonds had been on the wrong side of the hill in Alsace. There was no Thomas DeLion with the right dates buried anywhere in the Southwest. The search broadened, and came up with the discovery that a Thomas DeLion, a private first class in the United States Army during World War II, was buried in Morrill, Nebraska. And, it was later learned, Thomas DeLion was listed in a book on Nebraska's Forgotten Heroes.

With this certainty, Phil Tuckett, who was in the midst of producing a documentary on the quest for the diamonds for the Arts & Entertainment Network's History Channel, and his staff went on a search for Tommy DeLion's family. They found nothing in Nebraska, and, given Sam Nyer's certainty that Tommy was a Native American from a tribe in the Southwest, the hunt moved on to New Mexico and Arizona. That proved a dead end. The search then focused on the states surrounding Nebraska. It paid off. There were four families named DeLion in Kansas, and one of them, living in Ulysses, turned out to be that of Tommy's brother, Oliver. It was in conversation with Oliver that Tuckett heard that the DeLions were not, as Nyer and so many others believed, Native Americans, but a family of migrant workers from Mexico.

Tuckett, accompanied by Yaron Svoray, went to Ulysses, and fifty members of the DeLion family gathered in a hall provided by the local Veterans of Foreign Wars to hear the stories of the young man they had always considered a hero, even though they knew nothing about what he had done. They listened without a murmur to Svoray's recital of things he had heard from Nyer. When he told them about the diamonds, they seemed not to care, to have little interest in those stones. And then they gathered around a loudspeaker as the voice of Sam Nyer came through from his home in Bangor with his firsthand stories, things that he remembered about his best friend from the war. They could not hear enough, and kept asking questions, kept saying, "We knew he did something great."

On a bright, sunny day early in May 2002, Sam Nyer and his wife made the trip from Bangor to Morrill. They arrived early. The DeLion family was expected momentarily to take part in a memorial service. As Nyer reached the cemetery, he asked the superintendent for directions to Tommy's grave. The directions were a wave of the hand. "We'll have to find it ourselves," Nyer told his wife. They walked down the line of graves to one end of the cemetery when Nyer was overcome by a feeling that they were heading in the wrong direction. They turned and started back, moving down toward the other end, passing about forty graves. Suddenly, he stopped. A sense he could not describe overcame him. "You're standing on it," his wife said.

Nyer looked down. Just at his feet was the tombstone. "I looked down and saw it and began to cry," Nyer said. He kept staring down at the stone, at the carved name of Thomas DeLion. Then the DeLions arrived and gathered around. Nyer looked across at Tommy's brother, Oliver, and thought this was what Tommy might have become had he survived.

Nyer had survived the war, had come home, married, raised a family, lived a comfortable life, and grown old. Tommy DeLion had not survived and so, in Nyer's mind's eye, he would be always nineteen, forever young, eternally as he had been the last moment Nyer had seen him, a small, forlorn soldier standing beside a ruined foxhole in a forest on a hill in Alsace on a freezing February day in 1945.

In the years since then, Sam Nyer's life had been filled with two quests. The first was for the diamonds he and Tommy had buried in that foxhole, diamonds he was convinced had brought only bad luck, had been cursed. That quest he had ceded to Yaron Svoray, and Svoray and his friends had finally uncovered them. The second was to find Tommy or his grave and somehow try to come to terms with his death, put closure on the memories that had haunted him through half a century and more. Now he stood at the grave, feeling humbled, feeling grief-stricken, knowing there would be no closure, that the memories of Tommy would remain with him as long as he lived.

Then Sam Nyer left the cemetery to fly back to Maine.

Index